ASSEMBLY LANGUAGE INTERFACING IN TURBO PASCAL

Sanjiva Nath

Management Information Source, Inc.

COPYRIGHT

1107 N.W. 14th Avenue
Portland, Oregon 97209
(503) 222-2399

First Printing

ISBN 0-943518-25-3

Library of Congress Catalog Card Number: 87-5726

TABLE OF CONTENTS

INTRODUCTION

Assembly Language Interfacing in Turbo Pascal is designed for Turbo Pascal programmers wanting to extend the power of Turbo Pascal, which, as powerful as it is for small to medium-size applications, can be extended further as a program development tool by combining it with assembly language. Together with assembly language, Turbo Pascal is capable of almost any programming task.

In addition to being a powerful tool, Turbo Pascal also provides first-timers with a convenient environment in which to learn assembly language programming. You can start by writing small routines and let the Turbo Pascal compiler take care of establishing data structures, setting up the program environment, and interfacing with the operating system.

Essentially, you can learn assembly language one step at a time, first learning the instructions and addressing modes, and later you can learn the techniques for setting up the program environment and data structures in assembly language when you begin developing stand-alone assembly language applications.

The objective of this book is to make you literate in assembly language so that you can start writing small routines to interface with your Turbo Pascal programs. There is much more to programming in assembly language than what is presented here; however, not all information is necessary, especially if you are just beginning or if you only want to occasionally write small routines.

This book gives you the background on assembly language programming, covering the essentials. It discusses techniques for interfacing assembly language with Turbo Pascal using **Inline** machine code, **External** assembly language subroutines, as well as routines available through the PC's BIOS and DOS services. Finally, it also explores the opportunities for interfacing assembly language with Turbo Pascal, such as when accessing the PC's operating system and device I/O facilities—situations in which assembly language is almost indispensable and in which Turbo Pascal, being a high-level language, sometimes falters in performance.

Emphasis on the IBM PC is especially important in the context of Turbo Pascal's wide array of built-in services and low-level hooks that enable you to perform all kinds of wonderful programming techniques on the PC. To use some of these services, it is important not only to know the basics of Turbo Pascal and assembly language but also to know something about the IBM PC and the operating system environment in which it operates—PC DOS.

This book also explores the techniques for interfacing assembly language with Turbo Pascal. Programs are simple and demonstrative. By typing example programs in the Turbo Pascal editor, you can run the programs, alter them and run them again, and try your own ideas. Eventually, you will want to explore on your own, which is very much a part of learning, and no book can match that. *Assembly Language Interfacing in Turbo Pascal* presents simple and basic ideas while enticing you to reach beyond them and develop your own techniques.

Also, while parts of this book have been developed aound the IBM PC and PC DOS environment, you will most likely be able to use it just as effectively with a compatible running under MS DOS. As long as you can run Turbo Pascal in your system, you will be able to use this book.

Chapter Overviews

Chapter 1 begins with terms and concepts that are essential to assembly language programming. It discusses notations for representing data (decimal, hexadecimal, and binary), binary arithmetic, and two's complement. It also discusses how computer's store information and the difference between machine and assembly language.

Chapter 2 introduces you to Debug—a helpful utility that will prove invaluable to you if you indulge in assembly language programming. Among its many services, Debug allows you to trace step-by-step execution of a (compiled) Turbo Pascal program and peek and alter the contents of the computer's memory.

Chapter 3 traces a Turbo Pascal program in Debug while introducing the basic concepts related to the 8088 processor, such as the 8088 architecture, registers, flags, instruction pointer, addressing memory and I/O ports, and interrupts.

Chapter 4 discusses the operand addressing modes. An assembly language instruction may address an operand in a variety of ways, depending on the location and structure of the operand. Structured operands, such as arrays, tables, and records, entail rather complex addressing modes involving base and index registers

Chapters 5 and 6 present the 8088 assembly language instructions. These instructions are categorized into functional groups. The discussion is organized for both tutorial and reference. The commonly used instructions are discussed in detail.

Chapter 7 discusses the basic structure of machine code and the steps involved in converting assembly language into machine code. This conversion is analogous to the steps that an assembler takes in producing machine code from assembly language source code. This topic is of considerable interest to programmers who want to use machine code as inline statements in Turbo Pascal (or any other high-level language that allows inline machine code).

Chapter 8 focusses on the most preferred method for interfacing assembly language with Turbo Pascal—using Inline machine code.

Chapter 9 shows you how to call External assembly language subroutines from your Turbo Pascal programs. These routines may be part of a library of assembly language subroutines. Discussion also includes techniques involved in building a library of assembly language subroutines.

Chapter 10 discusses the easiest way to interface assembly language subroutines with Turbo Pascal programs—by invoking the prewritten and preassembled routines provided as part BIOS and DOS applications services.

Chapter 11 explores memory and disk file management on the IBM PC in PC-DOS. This discussion primarily focuses on how a Turbo Pascal program interfaces with the operating system environment.

Chapters 12 and 13 are dedicated to video display programming techniques. Discussion includes the basic theory behind the PC's video display and the PC's BIOS services available for manipulating text and graphics on the screen. Chapter 12 covers the text mode of the monochrome display and color graphics adapters. Chapter 13 covers the graphics mode of the Color Graphics Adapter.

Chapter 14 reviews the basics of how the keyboard works and how Turbo Pascal detects and reads keyboard input. Discussion also includes the BIOS and DOS services available for reading keyboard input.

Chapter 15 discusses techniques for writing interrupt service routines (ISR) in Turbo Pascal, using assembly language. The Ctrl-Break and DOS critical error interrupts are used as examples to build custom ISRs.

Again, the emphasis is on reading each chapter while practicing and exploring the example programs. The programs are short and simple because each one presents a single subroutine demonstrating various techniques and concepts. They are easy to follow and allow for a great deal of exploration. By putting together many such subroutines, you can easily create large applications.

Equipment Requirements

This book was primarily developed for an IBM PC system running under DOS 2.1 with at least 256K of memory, floppy and/or hard disk drives, monochrome or color display, and a parallel printer interface. Version 3.0 of Turbo Pascal was used. If you are using a clone, as long as you can run this version of Turbo Pascal on your system, you can also run the programs provided in this book.

Further Reading

You will find the following books quite useful when you begin exploring many of the topics introduced in this book:

Disk Operating System Technical Reference. Boca Raton, Florida: IBM Corporation, 1984.

Duncan, Ray. *Advanced DOS.* Bellevue, Washington: Microsoft Press, 1986.

Hyman, Michael. *Memory Resident Utilities, Interrupts, and Disk File Management With MS and PC DOS*. Portland, Oregon: MIS: Press, 1986.

iAPX 88 Book. Santa Clara, California: Intel Corp., 1983.

IBM Personal Computer Technical Reference. Boca Raton, Florida: IBM Corporation, 1984.

Morse, Stephen. *The 8086/8088 Primer*. Hasbrouck Heights, NJ: Hayden Book Company, 1982.

MS DOS Technical Reference Encyclopedia. Bellevue, Washington: Microsoft Press, 1986.

Norton, Peter. *Programmer's Guide To The IBM PC*. Bellevue, Washington: Microsoft Press, 1985.

Sargent, Murray, and Richard Shoemaker. *The IBM Personal Computer Inside Out*. Reading, Massachusetts: Addison-Wesley Publishing Company, 1984.

Scanlon, Leo. *IBM PC & XT Assembly Language—A Guide For Programmers*. New York, NY: Brady Communications Company, 1983.

Triebel, Walter and Avtar Singh. *The 8086 Microprocessor—Architecture, Software, and Interfacing Techniques*. Englewood Cliffs, NJ: Prentice-Hall, Inc., 1985.

Turbo Pascal User Reference Manual. Scotts Valley, CA: Borland International, 1985.

Graphics Primer for the IBM PC. Waite, Mitchell and Christopher L. Morgan. Berkely, CA: Osborne McGraw Hill, 1983.

CHAPTER 1

ESSENTIAL TERMS AND CONCEPTS

Before you can begin exploring assembly language interfacing in Turbo Pascal, you must know several terms and concepts that are closely associated with assembly language programming. You should also be familiar with some aspects of your computer system's hardware and architecture. This chapter contains a brief tutorial covering only the essential concepts. If you are already familiar with this information, you may want to proceed to the next chapter.

First, this chapter will discuss the ways computers represent and manipulate data. The following topics will be covered:

- notations for representing data: **decimal**, **binary**, and **hexadecimal**
- how computers store program instructions and data
- binary arithmetic
- machine versus assembly language

NOTATIONS FOR REPRESENTING DATA

Decimal Notation

Numbers are most often represented in **decimal** notation, i.e., the conventional numbering system in base 10. Decimal notation has ten digits—0 through 9—and the numbers progress in tens.

To represent numbers greater than nine in decimal notation, the following scheme is used.

The position of each digit in a number represents a power of 10 (10^n where $n=0$ for the rightmost digit and increases by 1 each digit to the left) as shown here:

$10^0=1$

$10^1=10$

$10^2=100$

$10^3=1000$

Therefore, it can be said that the position of a digit in a number determines its value or weight. A digit at the first (rightmost) position signifies ones; at the second position it signifies tens; at the third position it signifies hundreds; at the fourth position it signifies thousands of a value, and so on.

For example, you can show the breakdown of numbers 7, 47, and 147 as follows:

(7)

$$7 = 7 * 10^0$$

(47)

$$\begin{array}{rll} & 40 & (4 * 10^1) \\ + & 7 & (7 * 10^0) \\ \hline & 47 & \end{array}$$

(147)

$$\begin{array}{rll} & 100 & (1 * 10^2) \\ & 40 & (4 * 10^1) \\ + & 7 & (7 * 10^0) \\ \hline & 147 & \end{array}$$

Here, the rightmost digit represents 10 raised to the power of 0. The next digit represents 10 raised to the power of 1, and so on.

As you will see later in this chapter, this positional notation is equally significant in binary and hexadecimal notations.

Binary Notation

In contrast to conventional decimal notation, computers store and process data using **binary** notation. Binary refers to two; therefore, each **bit** (a combination of the words **bi**nary and digi**t**) of computer data can be represented as either of two digits, "0" or "1."

This representation of binary data in the form of 0's and 1's is quite arbitrary; you also see references to bits existing in one of two states, ON or OFF. Either way, the concept is the same.

In decimal notation, you have ten digits (0...9) with which to work. To express numbers greater than nine, you begin using multiple digits, as shown in the previous examples.

In contrast, binary notation provides only two digits (0, 1) with which to work; therefore, to express numbers greater than one, you must resort to using multiple digits. Each digit from right to left represents a power of 2 (2^n where n begins with 0 for the rightmost bit) as shown below:

$2^0 = 1$

$2^1 = 2$

$2^2 = 4$

$2^3 = 8$

$2^4 = 16$

$2^5 = 32$

$2^6 = 64$

$2^7 = 128$

$2^8 = 256$

You can now represent decimal 52 in binary notation as follows:

(52)

32	($\mathit{1} * 2^5$)
16	($\mathit{1} * 2^4$)
0	($\mathit{0} * 2^3$)
4	($\mathit{1} * 2^2$)
0	($\mathit{0} * 2^1$)
0	($\mathit{0} * 2^0$)
52	

These digits also conveniently represent the bit positions in a **byte**, as will be discussed later in this chapter; therefore, conventionally, you can express decimal 52 in binary as

		7 6 5 4 3 2 1 0 ←bit positions in a byte
52	=	***0 0 1 1 0 1 0 0***

Hexadecimal Notation

While binary notation may be convenient from the computer's perspective, it certainly isn't convenient for programmers. For example, look at the binary representation of a relatively small number such as 1004:

1004=001111101100

To make it easier to represent binary data in a format that remains compatible with binary notation, programmers devised the **hexadecimal** (or **hex**) notation in which numbers are represented in base 16. You will frequently see references to hex notation in this book as well as in many other books and programs.

In the hex format, there are 16 digits (decimal values ranging from 0 to 15). While this may not be difficult to understand, the unique characteristic of hex notation is the use of alpha characters to represent numbers greater than 9. Consider the following table which lists hex values for decimal numbers 0...17:

Table 1.1

Decimal	Hex
0	0
1	1
2	2
3	3
4	4
5	5
6	6
7	7
8	8
9	9
10	A
11	B
12	C
13	D
14	E
15	F
16	10
17	11

Perhaps the most difficult aspect of hex notation is the use of alpha characters as symbols. If you count to 16 before using double digits, you must use alpha characters in addition to the ten digits (0...9). Hex notation utilizes letters "A" through "F" to denote the numbers 10 through 16 respectively. It may look strange, but it works.

From left to right, each digit in hex notation represents a power of 16 (16^n where n begins with 0 for the rightmost bit) as shown here:

$16^0 = 1$

$16^1 = 16$

$16^2 = 256$

$16^3 = 4096$

$16^4 = 65536$

To represent numbers in hex notation, consider the following examples:

(hex 400 or decimal 1024)

1024	(*4* $* 16^2$)
0	(*0* $* 16^1$)
0	(*0* $* 16^0$)
1024	

(hex FFFF or decimal 65535)

61440	(*F* $* 16^3$)
3840	(*F* $* 16^2$)
240	(*F* $* 16^1$)
15	(*F* $* 16^0$)
65535	

To distinguish a hex number from a decimal number, you often follow the hex number by the letter "H," e.g., 1024H and FFFFH. In Turbo Pascal programs, however, hex numbers are represented with the "$" symbol as a prefix:

```
BufSize := $400;

DisplayBuf := $B800;
```

The "$" prefix will be used throughout this book to indicate hex numbers and to maintain compatibility with the Turbo format.

Needless to say, a thorough understanding of these notations is essential to programming in assembly language (or, for that matter, any language) if you want to access the PC's low-level facilities.

HOW COMPUTERS STORE INFORMATION

So far, you have examined ways data can be represented in programming. This section focuses on how computers store information such as program instructions and data.

The concept of bits and bytes is probably not unfamiliar to you, but it will be reviewed here briefly in an effort to build the necessary background picture.

In computer memory, data is stored in sequences of **bits**. A sequence of four bits is a **nibble**, and eight bits is a **byte**. Beyond that, a two-byte (16-bit) unit is sometimes referred to as a **word** and a four-byte (32-bit) unit as a **double word.** Consider these two definitions solely in the context of the IBM PC and the 8088 family of processors. Other processors (for example, the IBM 4300 series processors running large mainframe computers) may have 32-bit words and 64-bit double words. It is all arbitrary, based mostly on the unit of data that a particular processor can handle at a time.

A byte is the basic unit of computer memory used to store information. For this book's purposes, note that a byte is the smallest unit of data on which the PC's Central Processing Unit or **CPU** (the 8088 processor) can operate. A byte is also used to represent character data. As you will see, the entire extended ASCII character set is represented by a single byte.

Sometimes you may need to process large amounts of data. The term **block** is often used to signify a large array of contiguous memory cells. The actual size may depend on the particular application. For example, many communications programs transfer data in blocks of 128 or 256 bytes when using an error-correction protocol. This simply means that these programs send 128 or 256 bytes of data at a time.

BINARY ARITHMETIC

An important term in binary arithmetic is **two's complement**, a concept dealing with positive and negative binary numbers.

Two's complement is a special type of arithmetic used to indicate positive and negative numbers in the binary representation format. According to this arithmetic, the leftmost bit (the most significant bit or **MSB**) of a number represents its sign, and that bit is 0 if the number is positive and 1 if the number is negative.

In Turbo Pascal, the integer data type takes up two bytes in memory. Also, the maximum positive value represented by an integer data type in Turbo Pascal is 32767. The binary representation of this number is

    0111111111111111

If you were to force the eighth bit to a "1," the binary value in that integer would be

    1111111111111111

which is equivalent to decimal -1.

To understand two's complement, you must look at how it is created, i.e., how a positive binary number is converted into its corresponding negative value.

This is a two-step procedure:

1. Complement the number, i.e., convert all 1's to 0's and all 0's to 1's.

2. Add 1 to the complement.

For example, consider an integer value representing decimal 15:

15 = 0000000000001111

Its complement would then be

1111111111110000

and adding a 1 to that will yield

```
Complement    1111111111110000
              + 1
              ----------------
              1111111111110001
```

which is equivalent to decimal -15.

Similarly, when you want to change a negative number into a positive number, follow the same procedure:

```
-15 =         1111111111110001
Complement    0000000000001110
              + 1
              ----------------
              0000000000001111
```

which is equivalent to decimal 15.

Using the hexadecimal system, you can store values ranging from 0 to 65535 in an integer because hex FFFF is a positive number, and in operations related to large numbers such as memory addresses, you frequently encounter such values; however Turbo Pascal will see the integer value of hex FFFF (the unsigned format) as a -1 (the signed value). Therefore, when representing large numbers, you need to be aware of how they are treated by the Turbo Pascal compiler. Often, you will need a real variable to generate a positive result from the integer variable.

MACHINE VS. ASSEMBLY LANGUAGE

After reading this book, you will realize that another title for it could have been "Machine Language in Turbo Pascal" because, although both terms are often used interchangeably, machine language and assembly language are two different concepts, and what you will actually work with in this book is machine language code.

Here, the principal differences between the two languages will be discussed.

Earlier in this chapter, it was noted that the computer processes data in the form of bits that exist in one of two states—ON ("1") or OFF ("0"). Both programs and data are stored in memory in a sequence of 1's and 0's.

As you will see, the actual instructions are sequences of numbers, a unique sequence for each instruction. Even when compiled, Turbo Pascal programs are reduced to a series of numbers. Note that these numbers contain both instructions and data. They are collectively referred to as **machine code** or **machine language** since they represent the language that the machine (or computer) can understand.

While a program exists in memory as a series of numbers, for convenience, programmers have devised a way of representing individual instructions in a more readable form by using three and four-character mnemonics for these instructions.

Below are a few examples of instructions written in machine code and mnemonics:

Machine Code	Assembly Language
$B90400	MOV CX,$0004
$89C3	MOV BX,AX
$01D8	ADD AX,BX

It is obvious that a program written in machine code, as represented by the instructions on the left in the above examples, will be quite unreadable and difficult to maintain. Assembly language allows you to write more readable programs. When the assembly language code is translated into machine code by an **assembler**, there is a one-to-one correlation between each assembly language statement and machine code instruction; therefore, nothing is lost in translation.

In the next chapter, you will practice some of these concepts using the Debug program available with DOS diskettes. Debug has become quite valuable to programmers interested in learning assembly language.

CHAPTER 2

INTRODUCTION TO DEBUG

As a Turbo Pascal programmer about to enter the abstract world of machine and assembly language programming, you will find DOS's **Debug** utility to be quite valuable. Several commercial products offering more sophisticated features and functions are available; however, Debug is available for free (with a copy of DOS); it is easy to use, and it does the job. Again, if you have already used Debug, feel free to skip this section.

WHAT IS DEBUG?

Debug is a handy utility that allows you to interactively monitor and test your programs online. Debug provides the following principal services:

- Trace program execution step-by-step
- Peek at specified memory locations
- Peek at register values
- Alter contents of main memory
- Alter contents of a disk file
- Execute object files

Also, as stated earlier, Debug (file name DEBUG.COM) is provided with the DOS diskettes, generally on the Supplemental Program diskette.

WHY USE DEBUG?

Debug offers several advantages to Turbo Pascal users.

First, it is available for free, and second, it is easy to use. Most PC owners have a copy of Debug in their software library.

Third, when you begin using routines containing **inline** statements in Turbo Pascal programs, as you will see later in this book, you can use Debug to conveniently create and test them. Similarly, Debug is also convenient for testing **external** procedures created in assembly language and assembled using one of the available assemblers, such as MASM from Microsoft Corp.

STARTING WITH DEBUG

In this chapter, a few interactive sessions with Debug will be presented. The idea is for you to become familiar with its features and services. Call up Debug on your PC and type the example exercises as you read through this chapter. Each section will cover a single feature or service. At the end of each section, you can spend some time exploring what you have learned before moving on to the next section.

Also, if you have convenient access to the *DOS Reference Manual*, you may want to have it nearby for easy reference to Debug's commands and functions.

The first step is to bring up (execute) Debug. After you type in the program name at the DOS prompt, the Debug interpreter prompt appears:

```
C:\>debug          ← You type at the DOS prompt
-                  ← Debug's prompt
```

The dash here represents the cursor, which tells you that Debug is ready for input.

Note a few points about Debug before you begin:

- Debug is not case sensitive; therefore, you may use upper or lowercase letters.
- Function key <F3> repeats previous commands in Debug as it does in DOS.
- Debug's commands can be invoked by typing their first letter.

To exit Debug when you are finished, simply type "QUIT" at the prompt, and Debug will return you to DOS.

```
-quit              ← You type
C:\>               ← DOS prompt
```

Before exiting, however, try a few exercises.

DOING 'HEX' ARITHMETIC IN DEBUG

Debug's **H** (Hexarithmetic) command lets you perform simple arithmetic (addition and subtraction) on **hex** values. This can be a convenient tool for learning hex arithmetic as well as for actually using Debug to monitor and trace program execution.

Hexarithmetic expects two hex values as input and returns the sum and difference of the two values respectively on the next line, as shown here.

Example 2.1:

```
-h 2ad 1fe         ← You type
04AB  00AF         ← Debug responds
-
```

In this example, the second value is added to the first value to produce the sum, and it is subtracted from the first value to produce the difference on the second line.

You should also note that Debug, like Turbo Pascal, operates on two-byte (word) integer values. In the context of this discussion, when you add numbers that cause an overflow, Debug will truncate any high-order overflow digits.

The Hexarithmetic service will be used here to reinforce what you learned in Chapter 1 about hexadecimal notation and two's complement arithmetic.

Now try a few simple examples. A hex table has been provided in the Appendices for reference. You may want to use it when attempting calculations on your own before verifying the results using the Hexarithmetic command.

Remember, Debug is expecting and interpreting numbers in hex notation. In Example 2.2 below, 5 is added to 7 and 5 is subtracted from 7.

Example 2.2:

```
-h 7 5                ← You type
000C   0002           ← Debug responds
-
```

The two operations can be represented in decimal arithmetic as follows:

```
  7    7
 +5   -5
 12    2
```

You can see that the numbers do not change because decimal 5 is also hex 5, and decimal 7 is also hex 7.

The decimal-to-hex conversion for the results would be as follows:

12d = 0Ch
2d = 02h

Here, the suffix 'd' represents decimal (added only for clarity), and 'h' represents hex (common notation).

Example 2.3:

```
-h 1f b          ← You type
002A   0014      ← Debug responds
-
```

Now try to perform hex arithmetic on these numbers. One easy way is to convert these numbers into decimal and reconvert the result back into hex, as shown here:

```
  31 (1Fh)       31
+ 11 (0Bh)     - 11
  42 (2Ah)       20 (14h)
```

This conversion can be awkward when dealing with larger numbers. A more practical approach is to perform the conversion for digits in each column as you add or subtract, going right to left. Carryovers here apply the same way as they would in normal decimal arithmetic except that a carryover in hex notation occurs after 15 (after Fh) instead of after 9.

```
  1F        1F
+ 0B      - 0B
  2A        14
```

Starting with the rightmost column, first add Fh (decimal 15) to Bh (decimal 11) to get decimal 26. This sum can also be interpreted as a 10 (Ah) with a carryover (i.e., 1Ah). Add 1 to the next column and you get 2Ah.

Similarly, first subtract Bh (decimal 11) from Fh (decimal 15) and get 4. Then move left to the next column and subtract 0 from 1, leaving 1. The result is 14h.

Example 2.4:

```
-h 1fa 011          ← You type
020B   01E9         ← Debug responds
-
```

Now attempt to solve this problem directly in hex:

```
 1FA      1FA
+11      -11
 20B      1E9
```

If you look at the numbers above, you will realize that it is just as easy to perform arithmetic operations on hex numbers as on decimal numbers. It is not necessary to convert them to decimal numbers before you can add and subtract them. This is especially true for smaller numbers.

Example 2.5:

```
-h fec 1db          ← You type
11C7   0E11         ← Debug responds
-
```

Can you solve this problem directly in hex?

```
  FEC      FEC
+ 1DB     -1DB
  11C7     E11
```

If you are finding this solution difficult, remember that this method to add and subtract numbers is not the same one that you are familiar with. Therefore, this method will not come naturally to you. You may want to try some examples on paper before using Debug's calculator.

Two's Complement

Two's complement was discussed in Chapter 1. Here, a few exercises in two's complement arithmetic using Debug are presented.

You will recall from Chapter 1 that two's complement is a way of representing negative numbers. The 8088 processor recognizes the sign of integers from their high-order bit. When this bit is a "1," the number is negative, and when it is a "0," the number is positive. The two's complement notation allows you to represent negative numbers with the high-order bit turned on ("1"). You get a two's complement number by reversing the bit values of a number and adding 1 to the result.

Consider a few examples of two's complement arithmetic.

Example 2.6:

```
-h 5 7              ← You type
000C   FFFE         ← Debug responds
-
```

Knowing two's complement notation, you should not be surprised at the results in Example 2.6. First, by looking at the high-order bit (F = 1111) of the second number, you can easily tell that it is a negative number (which is what you expect since 5 - 7 = -2).

Second, if you convert this number into its binary form, complement it, and add 1 to it, you should expect to get the binary form of 2:

FFFE =	1111 1111 1111 1110	← decimal -2
	0000 0000 0000 0001	← its complement
+	1	← adding 1
	0000 0000 0000 0010	← decimal +2

Another way of verifying that FFFE represents -2 is by adding it to +2 and subtracting it from +2. The results should be 0 and 4 respectively.

+2 - 2 = 0
+2 - (-2) = 4

Example 2.7:

```
-h 2 FFFe        ← You type
0000  0004       ← Debug responds
-
```

If you want more practice with two's complement, continue with some of your own exercises before moving on.

PEEKING AT THE COMPUTER'S MEMORY: DUMP AND UNASSEMBLE

In this section, you will look at two of Debug's commands used most frequently in this book to examine the contents of memory locations. These commands are **Dump** and **Unassemble**.

Dump Memory

Debug's **Dump** command allows you to peek at specified memory locations. You can either specify the memory address or the range, starting at a specific memory address where you want to examine the contents.

Dump produces a "dump" on the screen of the specified range in both hexadecimal and ASCII (readable or printable) formats, as shown in Figure 2.1.

```
---------------------------------------------------------------------------
C:\wp1>debug
-d 000:000
0000:0000  72 30 EB 00 47 01 70 00-C3 E2 00 F0 47 01 70 00   r0k.G.p.Cb.pG.p.
0000:0010  47 01 70 00 54 FF 00 F0-47 FF 00 F0 47 FF 00 F0   G.p.T..pG..pG..p
0000:0020  EB 08 33 09 7C 0A 33 09-DD E6 00 F0 DD E6 00 F0   k.3.|.3.]f.p]f.p
0000:0030  DD E6 00 F0 4E 08 00 C8-57 EF 00 F0 47 01 70 00   ]f.pN..HWo.pG.p.
0000:0040  DF 0F 33 09 4D F8 00 F0-41 F8 00 F0 08 0A 33 09   _.3.Mx.pAx.p..3.
0000:0050  39 E7 00 F0 59 F8 00 F0-A3 0A 33 09 D2 EF 00 F0   9g.pYx.p#.3.Ro.p
0000:0060  00 00 00 F6 B0 01 00 C8-6E FE 00 F0 F2 00 68 05   ...v0..Hn~.pr.h.
0000:0070  C4 08 33 09 A4 F0 00 F0-22 05 00 00 00 00 00 F0   D.3.$p.p"......p
---------------------------------------------------------------------------
```

Figure 2.1 Debug's Dump Command

Figure 2.1 is an example of the memory dump that Debug will display on the screen, which is a "dump" of low memory, starting at address absolute zero. Each double word (four bytes) in this area contains a memory address. Since this address points a program to a specified location in memory, it serves as a "pointer" or "vector." These vectors will be examined in more detail later in the book.

The next chapter discusses memory addressing conventions on the PC and also shows you how to read the memory addresses displayed in this dump. For now, just remember the command used to display contents of memory.

Unassemble Memory

Similar to Dump, Debug's **Unassemble** also allows you to examine the contents of memory; however, in contrast to Dump, Unassemble translates the contents of memory into assembly language instructions, displaying both the assembly language mnemonics as well as machine code.

An example of Unassemble is presented in the next section when you take an inside look at a Turbo Pascal program.

PEEKING AT A TURBO PASCAL PROGRAM

Since debug cannot read your Turbo Pascal source code files, you need to compile a program on disk and then load it into Debug.

Execute your Turbo Pascal compiler, and type the following program. The compiled program file will be referred to as TURBOASM.COM. You may call it whatever you want, as long as you know which file is being referred to in this book.

Program 2.1

```
/* ------------------------------------------------------------ */
/* Program 2-1                        2/26/87                   */
/* Author: Sanjiva Nath               Version 1                 */
/*                                                              */
/* Description: A simple Turbo Pascal program to               */
/* demonstrate Debug's facilities.                              */
/* ------------------------------------------------------------ */

program TurboAsm;
var
  X,Y : integer;

begin
   Inline($90/$90/$90);    { three NOP instruction }

   X := 9;
   Y := X * X;

  Inline($90/$90/$90);
end.
```

Once you have typed this program, compile it to make sure there aren't any compiling errors introduced while typing the program. If the compiled program is error free, compile it to disk as a .COM file and exit Turbo Pascal.

There are two ways to execute Debug and load TURBOASM.COM into memory:

1. By specifying the file name as Debug's command line parameter:

```
C:\>debug turboasm.com
```

2. By loading the file in Debug:

```
-n turboasm.com          ← set file name to be used by load
-l                       ← load file
-
```

Turbo's Inline Statement

First, your objective is to load a Turbo Pascal program into memory and monitor it with Debug. Comparing the size of the source file (100+ bytes) with that of the object file (11000+ bytes), you know that the compiled Turbo Pascal program consists of more than the four statements you typed in the TURBOASM.PAS file. The rest of the program will be covered later. For now, you need something to mark the location where you want Debug to begin monitoring the program. This is best accomplished by inserting a few dummy instructions of your own into the program prior to the marked location. With Debug, you can search for the dummy instructions and trace the program from there.

Turbo's **inline** statement allows you to do just that. Chapter 8 discusses the Inline statement. For now, think of it as a tool for inserting machine instructions into the program.

Tracing a Turbo Pascal Program

In this program, three **NOP** instructions have been inserted just before and after the two Pascal program statements. NOP is always a great instruction to learn first since it does nothing (**No** **Op**eration). Inserting three NOPs into the program will help you identify the spot, since it is unlikely that the compiler will code three NOPs in a sequence in the program.

The program is simple and limited to two statements so that you can trace the two instructions and gain some understanding of how the Turbo Pascal compiler translates program statements into machine executable code.

Now, return to Debug and begin tracing the program.

First, type "U" at the prompt to unassemble the contents of memory at the start of the program. The screen should resemble Figure 2.2.

```
-----------------------------------------------------------------------------
D:\turbopas>debug
-n turboasm.com
-l
-u
26AE:0100 E9792C        JMP     2D7C
26AE:0103 90            NOP
26AE:0104 90            NOP
26AE:0105 CDAB          INT     AB
26AE:0107 43            INC     BX
26AE:0108 6F            DB      6F
26AE:0109 7079          JO      0184
26AE:010B 7269          JB      0176
26AE:010D 67            DB      67
26AE:010E 68            DB      68
26AE:010F 7420          JZ      0131
26AE:0111 284329        SUB     [BP+DI+29],AL
26AE:0114 2031          AND     [BX+DI],DH
26AE:0116 3938          CMP     [BX+SI],DI
26AE:0118 352042        XOR     AX,4220
26AE:011B 4F            DEC     DI
26AE:011C 52            PUSH    DX
26AE:011D 4C            DEC     SP
26AE:011E 41            INC     CX
26AE:011F 4E            DEC     SI
-----------------------------------------------------------------------------
```

Figure 2.2 Unassembling in Debug

Since the program was just loaded into memory, the unassemble command is operating at the start of the program with the first instruction at the top. In Figure 2.2, the first instruction—JMP 2D7C—is a jump to a specific memory location (2D7C - 100 bytes from the current location).

To get to the NOPs, use Debug's **Search** command to search for a string of three NOPs in the program memory, as shown here.

```
-s cs:100 ffff 90 90 90         — search parameters
1BB5:2D9F                       — the first encounter
1BB5:2DB2                       — the second encounter
-
```

The search parameters specify to Debug that you want to begin the search from the current location (at the top of the program) to (FFFF - 100) bytes from current location, and the search is for a triple occurrence of machine code 90 (which is the NOP instruction). Debug returns the addresses of all occurrences of this string within the specified range.

Since there are only two occurrences in the program (before and after the program statements), you should not expect any more.

Jump to the first NOP instruction by changing to the new value the value of the **instruction pointer** (IP), which points at the current instruction to be executed.

```
-rip        ← requesting the current value of IP
IP 0100     ← Debug returns 0100
:2d9f       ← Debug requests new value
-           ← IP is set to new value following input
```

Now, try to unassemble the program starting at the first NOP to see if it can be interpreted. See Figure 2.3.

```
--------------------------------------------------------------------------
D:\turbopas>debug turboasm.com
-n turboasm.com
-l
-s cs:100 ffff 90 90 90
26AE:2D9F
26AE:2DB2
-rip
IP 0100
:2d9f
-u 2d9f
26AE:2D9F 90            NOP
26AE:2DA0 90            NOP
26AE:2DA1 90            NOP
26AE:2DA2 B80900        MOV     AX,0009
26AE:2DA5 A36002        MOV     [0260],AX
26AE:2DA8 A16002        MOV     AX,[0260]
26AE:2DAB F72E6002      IMUL    WORD PTR [0260]
26AE:2DAF A36202        MOV     [0262],AX
26AE:2DB2 90            NOP
26AE:2DB3 90            NOP
26AE:2DB4 90            NOP
26AE:2DB5 E90000        JMP     2DB8
26AE:2DB8 33C0          XOR     AX,AX
26AE:2DBA E8CCDE        CALL    0C89
26AE:2DBD 0000          ADD     [BX+SI],AL
--------------------------------------------------------------------------
```

Figure 2.3 Unassembling a Turbo Pascal Program in Debug

Each line displayed by Unassemble represents a machine instruction. You will notice the NOP instruction strings that sandwich five instructions. These five instructions represent the two program statements, which should give you some idea of why most people prefer using a high-level language like Pascal rather than assembly language or machine code. It is easier to represent certain operations in Pascal-like syntax rather than in assembly language machine code.

Look at the five instructions to see how they correspond with the two program statements:

Pascal Program Statements:

```
1.   X := 9;
2.   Y := X * X;
```

Assembly language (Debug) Program Statements:

```
1.   mov     ax,9
     mov     [260],ax

2.   mov     ax,[260]
     imul    word ptr [260]
     mov     [262],ax
```

You can use Debug's **Trace** command to trace through these five instructions. The value specified in square brackets is the offset to the data segment register. To find the value at that location, use the following command line parameters in Debug:

```
-d ds:0262
```

Note that the integer variable X resides at locations DS:0260 and DS:261 (two bytes), and Y resides at locations DS:262 and DS:263. By peeking at these locations at different times during the trace, you can gain insight into how data is actually moved, stored, and operated upon in the computer. A simple assignment statement actually becomes a two-step process. Similarly, it takes three instructions to perform a multiplication.

This exercise in tracing a Turbo Pascal program should prove valuable to you throughout this book. When you add inline code to your programs, the easiest way to trace the execution of the instructions embedded in the inline code is to mark them with a series of NOPs and use Debug to directly branch to those instructions. Later, when reggisters, flags, instruction pointers, and other entities related to the 8088 processor as well as memory addressing notations are discussed, you will be better able to understand their significance.

DEBUG COMMAND SUMMARY

In this section, Debug's commands are summarized for your convenience. For more details, refer to the section on Debug in the *DOS Reference Manual.*

Assemble

Allows you to input assembly language instructions directly into memory. Debug assembles them one instruction at a time. The standard 8086/8088 assembly language syntax is supported for entering instructions.

Compare

Compares the contents of two specified areas (blocks) of memory, and returns the addresses and contents of the unmatched areas.

Dump

Displays the contents of memory in ASCII (printable) and hexadecimal formats.

Enter

Allows you to alter the contents of memory at specific locations.

Fill

Fills a range of memory with specified data.

Go

Executes current program in memory until it terminates normally or, alternatively, until a user-set breakpoint is reached.

Hexarithmetic

Adds and subtracts two hexadecimal values.

Input

Reads and displays a byte from the specified port.

Load

Loads a file (or specific sectors) from disk into memory.

Move

Copies the contents of one specified range of memory location to another.

Name

Sets up File Control Blocks (FCB's) for use with Load and Write commands, and supplies file names for programs being debugged.

FCB's will be discussed in a later chapter, along with disk file management in DOS.

Output

Writes a byte to the specified port.

Proceed

Causes Debug to step through the execution of a subroutine call, a loop, an interrupt, or a repeat string instruction.

Quit

Exits Debug and returns to DOS.

Register

Displays the current contents of the registers and flags. It also allows you to alter the contents of specific registers.

Search

Searches the memory range for a specified string of data.

Trace

Traces the execution of a program one step at a time.

Unassemble

Translates memory contents into assembly language statements.

Write

Writes the data being debugged to a disk file.

CHAPTER 3

AN 8088/8086 PRIMER

TRACING A TURBO PASCAL PROGRAM IN DEBUG

You do not need to know the intricate details associated with the 8088/8086 microprocessors to be able to program in Turbo Pascal on the IBM PC and other compatible MS-DOS-based computers; however, when you begin interfacing assembly language code into your Turbo Pascal programs, you will come across several concepts that are related to the microprocessor's architecture, data structures, memory addressing modes, and input/output facilities.

This chapter familiarizes you with a few basic concepts related to the 8088. The following topics are covered:

- The 8088 architecture
- Registers, Flags, and the Instruction Pointer
- Memory addressing
- Addressing I/O ports
- Interrupts

In this and subsequent chapters, Debug will occasionally be referred to to illustrate a few points. You may want to review Chapter 2, especially the Debug command summary provided at the end of the chapter, before beginning this section.

THE 8088 ARCHITECTURE

The IBM PC and similar models are driven by the 8088 or compatible (such as the NEC V20) microprocessor. This chip belongs to the large family of processors, its closest cousin being the 8086.

The 8088 has four sets of 13 internal 16-bit registers. It is capable of addressing a total of 1024K bytes of memory and 64K of I/O ports.

REGISTERS, FLAGS, AND THE INSTRUCTION POINTER

As stated earlier, the 8088 microprocessor has several data structures called **registers**, which are used to store and process numbers. These registers are 16 bits (one word) wide, although some of them can also be accessed as 8-bit (half-word or byte) structures.

Registers are special memory locations that are part of the 8088 microprocessor. When the 8088 needs to process numbers, it brings those numbers into specific registers. Similarly, when memory addresses are calculated, the processor looks at specific registers to determine the absolute address. And, finally, there is even a register that keeps track of the program instruction to be executed.

A total of 13 word-sized registers are available to you. Their functional breakdown is as follows:

1. Data registers—AX, BX, CX, and DX

2. Pointer registers—BP and SP

3. Index registers—SI and DI

4. Segment registers—ES and DS

5. Instruction pointer register—IP

6. Status register (also Flag register)

Data Registers

As the name states, the data registers are used to store and process data items. Data registers are four 16-bit registers, and they are also available as eight 8-bit registers as shown here in Figure 3.1.

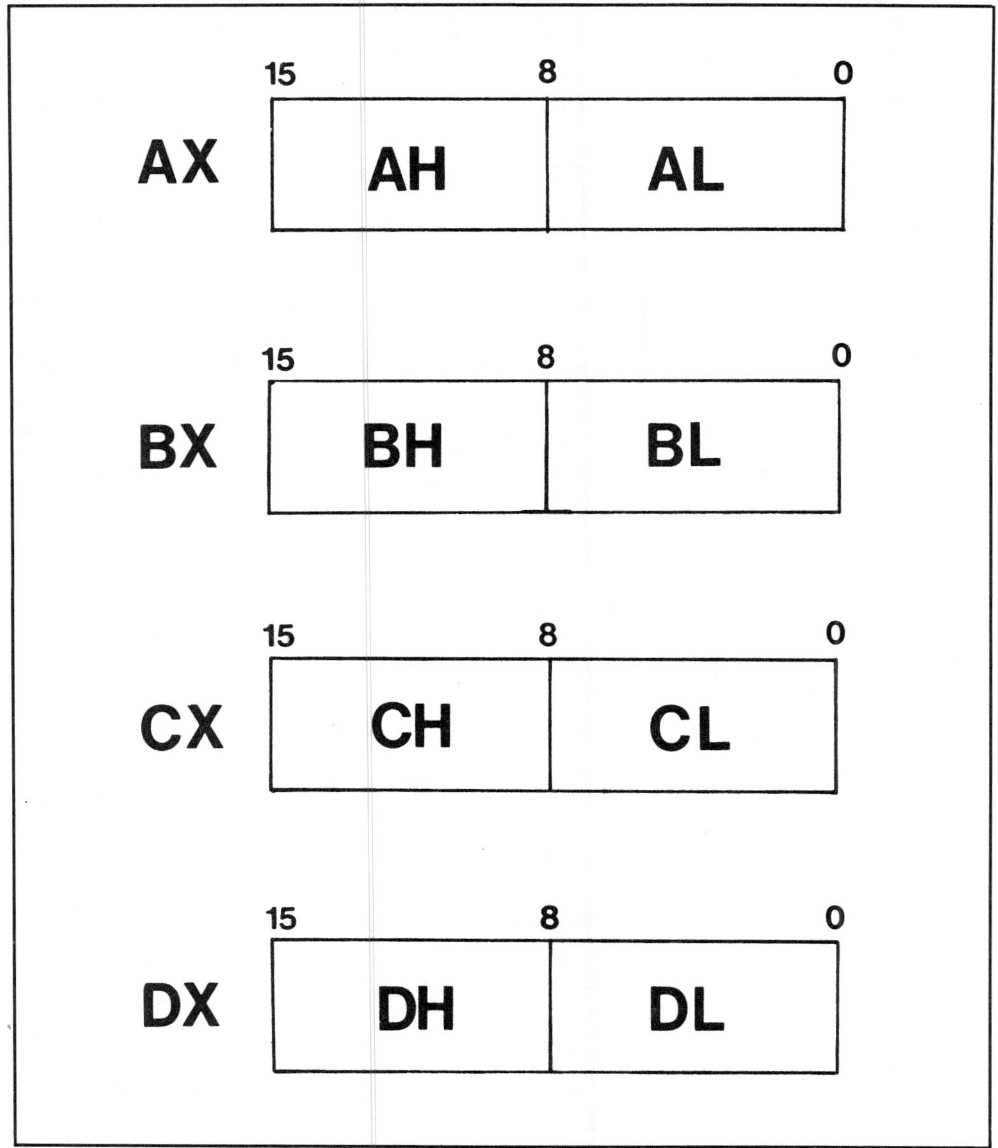

Figure 3.1 General Purpose Registers

Note that the suffix "H" signifies the high-order byte, and "L" signifies the low-order byte of the 16-bit register.

The reason for this 8-bit/16-bit personality for these data registers is perhaps to maintain compatability with the 8-bit world while introducing the advanced design associated with the 8086 microprocessor (8088's bigger brother).

In any case, just remember that the size of a register accessed in an instruction depends on the way it is addressed in that instruction. For example, if you refer to the AH register, you are referring to the high-order byte of the AX register, and you can only move byte-size data items into it.

The data registers are general purpose registers that may be used for a wide variety of functions. The **AX register** is also often referred to as the **accumulator** because it retains some of the functions of the old accumulator. In the older generation of microprocessors, a single register—the accumulator—was the center of arithmetic and logical operations, and data was moved into the accumulator from memory, processed, and moved back into memory.

In the 8088, the AX still plays a significant role, although its functions have been somewhat distributed over to the other three registers—BX, CX, and DX. Many instructions still require that the data item to be processed first be moved into the AX register. These instructions are covered in Chapter 5.

The **BX register** is often used as a base register in some memory addressing schemes. Examples of these schemes are in Chapter 4, where you will look at the various memory segmentation and addressing modes of the 8088.

The **CX register** is often used as a loop counter. In Chapter 6, you will look at examples of some instructions that actually require specific counts to be stored in the CX register.

Similarly, the **DX register** is often used to store 16-bit data. It is also used as an extension of the AX register when you need a 32-bit structure for performing multiplications and divisions.

Pointer and Index Registers

The two pointer registers—**BP (base pointer)** and **SP (stack pointer)**—are both used to point to the **stack**, a structure that is frequently used to pass parameters to subroutines and back, store return addresses from subroutines, and save register values for later retrieval.

The BP is available to the program for use in locating specific data items on the stack. It can be used independently of the stack pointer register.

The index registers—**SI (source index)** and **DI (destination index)**—are used in complex addressing modes. Several string manipulation instructions also use them. In this respect, they have special auto-incrementing and auto-decrementing capabilities (see Direction Flag later in this chapter).

Segment Registers

The segment registers are used to identify the various memory segments that contain the program, data, stack, and other structures as required and used by a program. They may all be the same, i.e., a single segment is used for program, data, and stack. They may also be overlapping or altogether separate. The memory organization depends primarily on how a program sets it up. Memory organization of a Turbo Pascal program will be discussed later in this section.

The 8088 has four segment registers—CS, DS, SS, and ES.

The **CS (Code Segment) register** identifies the segment in which the program (code) resides. Absolute memory addresses of specific instructions are calculated by combining the segment address in the CS register with the offset address in the **Instruction Pointer (IP)** to get a 20-bit absolute address of the instruction—CS:IP.

Later in this section, when a Turbo Pascal program is traced in Debug, examine the values in the CS and IP. You will notice that the IP changes with each step, whereas the CS remains constant because the instructions you are tracing all reside in the same code segment.

The **DS (Data Segment) register** identifies the segment in which the data (program variables) reside. In conjunction with another register containing the offset of a particular data structure (for example DS:BX), this register can also be used to find the absolute memory address of that data structure.

The **SS (Stack Segment) register** points to the stack segment. It is used in conjunction with the Stack Pointer (SP) register discussed earlier (SS:SP). It is also often used in conjunction with the Base Pointer register (BP) to access specific data items on the stack.

The **ES (Extra Segment) register** points to an extra segment of memory if set up and used in the program. Many string instructions use the DS and ES registers to mark the source and destination of string moves.

Instruction Pointer Register

The **instruction pointer register** holds the offset address of the next instruction to be executed. This offset is applied to the current segment address to calculate the absolute address of that instruction in memory. As you may have guessed, the CS register holds the value of the current segment.

During sequential processing, with the execution of each instruction, the value of the IP is automatically updated, based on the size of the instruction. For example, execution of the NOP instruction will cause the IP to be incremented by one because NOP is only one byte long.

Similarly, IP is updated every time a branch occurs in either direction to some other instruction in memory. In this case, the IP's contents are replaced by the offset address of the new instruction. While this type of branching is within the segment (**intrasegment**), both CS and IP are also updated if the branch occurs outside the current segment (**intersegment**).

Later in this chapter, you will trace another simple Turbo Pascal program using Debug. Notice the value in the IP each time an instruction is executed. You will also see an example of an intrasegment branch during this trace.

Status Register

The status register is functionally a collection of bits that indicate the outcome of certain arithmetic and logical operations. These individual bits (nine in all) are often referred to as **flags** and the status register referred to as the **flag register**. For convenience of addressing these bits in instructions, they have been equated with their functional names, as shown in Figure 3.2. These bits (or flags) will be discussed briefly here, starting with the least significant (rightmost) bit—bit 0.

More details on these flags are provided in the next chapter in the context of specific instructions that manipulate them.

Carry flag (CF)—Used in arithmetic calculations, bit 0 of the status register indicates if an addition between two 16-bit numbers has produced a carry or, conversely, a borrow as a result of subtraction. The processor sets the bit to a one for both situations, so the context in which this flag is read is important in determining what it indicates.

Parity flag (PF)—Used primarily in data communications, bit 2 of the status register tests the result for parity. The bit is set to a one if the parity is even, i.e., the number of one bits is even. Conversely, it is set to zero if the resulting value has an odd number of one bits.

This flag can be used to set the parity bit to make the parity even or odd, depending on the type of communications protocol desired. The parity flag is also of little use in arithmetic and logical operations.

For more on odd/even parity, refer to communications in Chapter 14.

Auxiliary carry flag (AF)—Bit 4 of the status register is used primarily in **Binary Coded Decimal (BCD)** arithmetic.

Zero flag (ZF)—Bit 6 of the status register is set to a one if the result of an operation is zero. A comparison, for example, may set ZF to a one if two values being compared are the same, i.e., the result of subtracting one from the other is zero.

Sign flag (SF)—Bit 7 of the status register is set to a one if the result of an arithmetic or logical operation is negative. This bit reflects the high-order bit of the resulting value. As discussed in Chapter 1, the high-order bit indicates the sign of signed numbers, and the number is negative if this bit is set to a one (two's complement arithmetic).

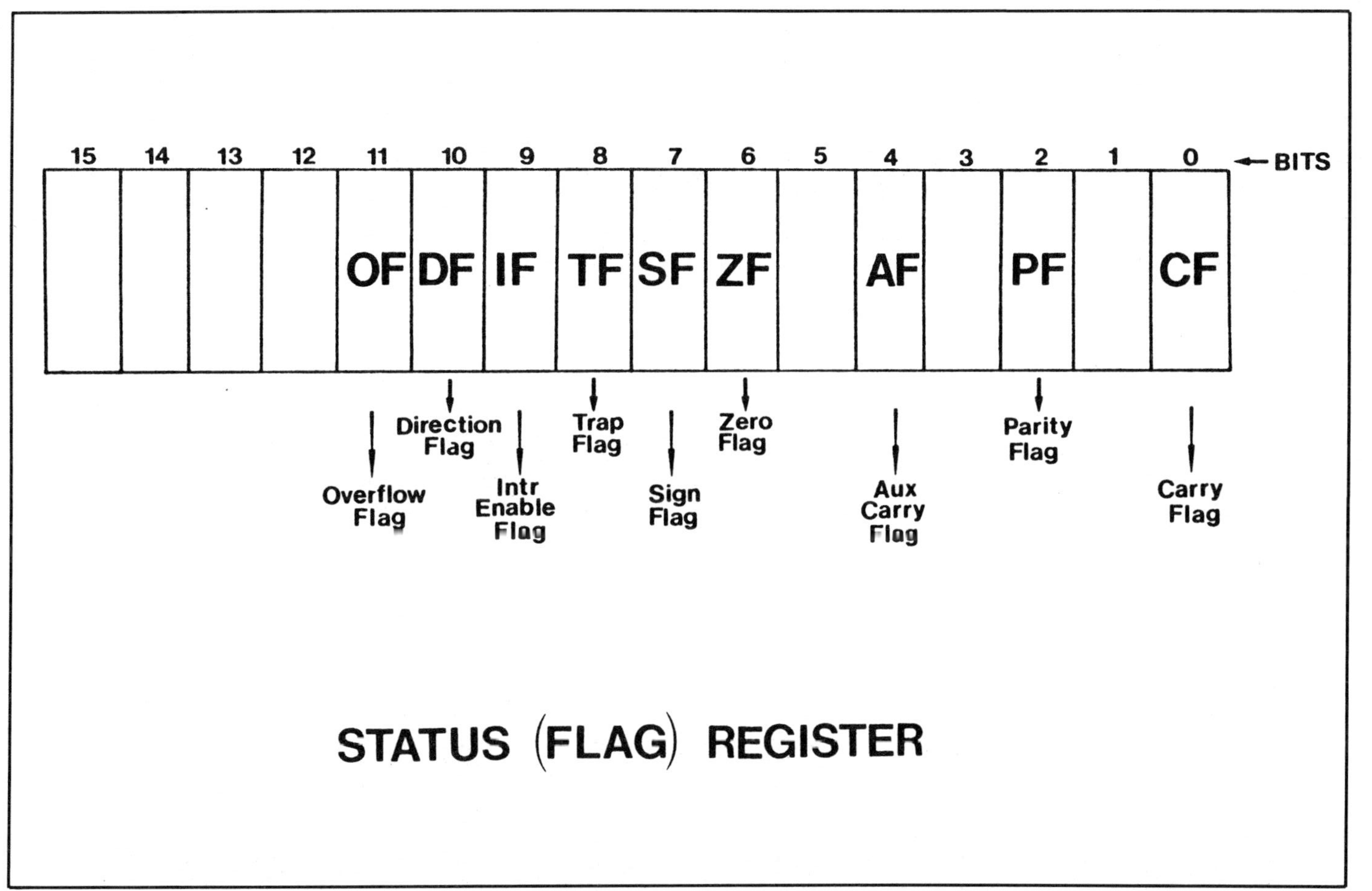

Figure 3.2 Status Register

Trap flag (TF)—Bit 8 of the status register is used for debugging purposes and causes the processor to single-step through the program instructions. This flag is set by the program and not as a result of any operation. Its effect is similar to an interrupt occurring after every instruction. A discussion of interrupts follows later in this chapter.

Interrupt enable flag (IF)—A program can cause the processor to either ignore or recognize external interrupts, depending on the setting of bit 9 of the status register. If the flag is set to a zero, the processor ignores all external interrupts.

Direction flag (DF)—Bit 10 of the status register dictates the direction (forward or backward) in which the 8088 processes a string. This bit functions in the context of string instructions that process large arrays of data. The setting of this flag causes the index register to be incremented or decremented by one.

Overflow flag (OF)—Bit 11 of the status register primarily indicates an error condition (overflow) in arithmetic operations using signed numbers.

The remaining bits of the status register stay unused. Chapters 5 and 6 will describe in more detail how instructions manipulate and are influenced by specific bit settings of the status register. You will also look at specific instructions provided for reading and setting these bit flags.

Peeking at a Register in Debug

Now that you have gained a basic familiarity and understanding of the 8088 registers, you can peek at them using Debug. Execute Debug as discussed in Chapter 2, and when you see the familiar prompt "-", type "r" and press <Enter>. You will receive a response similar (perhaps not identical) to the one in Figure 3.3.

Figure 3.3 illustrates the outcome of Debug's **Register** command. As mentioned in Chapter 2 in Debug's command summary, the Register command causes Debug to display the contents of all the registers and status flags, as well as the current instruction (ADD) to be executed.

You can ignore the instruction at this point because you have not loaded any program into memory. The ADD instruction is a side effect caused by the presence of hex 0's in the memory location where the instruction pointer is set.

Notice the emphasis on hex notation. You must have at least a working knowledge of the hex notation, especially when working with assembly language.

```
C>debug
-r
AX=0000  BX=0000  CX=0000  DX=0000  SP=00EE  BP=0000  SI=0000  DI=0000
DS=7379  ES=7379  SS=7379  CS=7379  IP=0100   NV UP EI PL NZ NA PO NC
7379:0100 0000          ADD     [BX+SI],AL
DS:0000=CD
-
```

Figure 3.3 Register Values in Debug

The Register command also lets you alter the contents of specific registers. To alter the contents of AX, for example, type

```
rax
```

at the prompt. Debug will display the value of the AX register, and ask for a new value. At this point type 1AD and press <Enter> as shown in Figure 3.4.

```
-rax
AX 0000
:1ad
-r
AX=01AD  BX=0000  CX=0000  DX=0000  SP=00EE  BP=0000  SI=0000  DI=0000
DS=7379  ES=7379  SS=7379  CS=7379  IP=0100   NV UP EI PL NZ NA PO NC
7379:0100 0000          ADD     [BX+SI],AL                   DS:0000=CD
```

Figure 3.4 Altering Register Contents

Now, if you want to explore the registers and their role in processing various instructions, type the following program in your Turbo Pascal Editor, compile it to disk, and load the compiled program into Debug. You will then trace through a few instructions to see how their execution affects the registers in real time.

Program 3.1

```
/* ------------------------------------------------ */
/* Program 3-1                      2/30/87          */
/* Author: Sanjiva Nath             Version 1        */
/*                                                   */
/* Description: A simple Turbo Pascal program to     */
/* demonstrate Debug's trace facilities and registers */
/* ------------------------------------------------ */

program TurboAsm;
var
  X,Y,Z : byte;

begin
   Inline($90/$90/$90);

   X := 10;
   Y := 5;
   repeat
     Y := Y + 1
   Until  (Y = X);
   Z := Y DIV X;

  Inline($90/$90/$90);
end.
```

Figure 3.5 suggests the steps that you will take to begin tracing the program after executing Debug. After specifying the new file name, instruct Debug to load the program into memory. Following that command, you want to search for the location marked by the three NOPs. You then set the instruction pointer to the first NOP. Type

```
t
```

for "trace" at the prompt, and Debug will display the next instruction in the queue to be executed and the current register contents.

```
C:\>debug
-n d:\turbopas\turboasm.com
-l
-s cs:100 ffff 90 90 90
738F:2D9F
738F:2DE2
-rip
IP 0100
:2d9f
-t

AX=0000  BX=0000  CX=2D27  DX=0000  SP=FFEE  BP=0000  SI=0000  DI=0000
DS=738F  ES=738F  SS=738F  CS=738F  IP=2DA0   NV UP EI PL NZ NA PO NC
738F:2DA0 90            NOP
-
```

Figure 3.5 Tracing in Debug

Bypass the three NOPs (type "t" one more time) and look at the next few instructions using the Unassemble command. These instructions are illustrated in Figure 3.6 and will be discussed in Chapters 5 and 6. Here, they will only be used to illustrate the roles registers play in your programs.

Note that the program instructions were actually coded in Turbo Pascal. What you are about to trace is Turbo Pascal's compilation in machine code, as unassembled by Debug's "unassembler."

Following the "unassembly," you will also trace a single instruction to display the registers. This instruction is represented in Figure 3.7.

```
-u
738F:2DA2 B80A00        MOV     AX,000A
738F:2DA5 A26002        MOV     [0260],AL
738F:2DA8 B80500        MOV     AX,0005
738F:2DAB A26102        MOV     [0261],AL
738F:2DAE A06102        MOV     AL,[0261]
738F:2DB1 32E4          XOR     AH,AH
738F:2DB3 050100        ADD     AX,0001
738F:2DB6 A26102        MOV     [0261],AL
738F:2DB9 A06102        MOV     AL,[0261]
738F:2DBC 32E4          XOR     AH,AH
738F:2DBE 50            PUSH    AX
738F:2DBF A06002        MOV     AL,[0260]
-u
738F:2DC2 32E4          XOR     AH,AH
738F:2DC4 59            POP     CX
738F:2DC5 91            XCHG    CX,AX
738F:2DC6 3BC1          CMP     AX,CX
738F:2DC8 7403          JZ      2DCD
738F:2DCA E9E1FF        JMP     2DAE
738F:2DCD A06102        MOV     AL,[0261]
738F:2DD0 32E4          XOR     AH,AH
738F:2DD2 50            PUSH    AX
738F:2DD3 A06002        MOV     AL,[0260]
738F:2DD6 32E4          XOR     AH,AH
738F:2DD8 59            POP     CX
738F:2DD9 91            XCHG    CX,AX
738F:2DDA 99            CWD
738F:2DDB F7F9          IDIV    CX
738F:2DDD A26202        MOV     [0262],AL
```

Figure 3.6 Debug's Unassembly

The instructions that appear in Figure 3.6 are the result of Turbo Pascal statements sandwiched between the NOP's in Program 3.1. From left to right, the first column displays the address of each instruction in the segment:offset format. The offset of the current instruction (the instruction at the top) can also be read in the instruction pointer (see Figure 3.7).

The next column in Figure 3.6 represents the machine code for each instruction. Depending on the specific instruction, the actual machine code may be one or several bytes in size.

The rightmost columns represent the assembly language statements corresponding to the machine code. These statements consist of the instruction mnemonics and one or more parameters.

The numbers in square brackets represent offset addresses of byte variables X, Y, and Z in the program. The actual addresses are calculated by adding the offset to the value in the data segment; therefore, X will be at DS:[0260] or 738F:0260.

```
-t

AX=000A  BX=0000  CX=2D2B  DX=0000  SP=FFEE  BP=0000  SI=0000  DI=0000
DS=738F  ES=738F  SS=738F  CS=738F  IP=2DA5   NV UP EI PL NZ NA PO NC
738F:2DA5 A26002        MOV     [0260],AL                   DS:0260=41
```

Figure 3.7 Single-Stepping through Debug

Figure 3.7 represents Debug's display after single-stepping through the first instruction following the NOP's:

```
MOV       AX,000A
```

This instruction moves the value 0Ah into the AX register. Since this instruction has been executed, you can see the value 0Ah (decimal 10) in the AX register. (Actually, it is in the AL register.)

The next instruction in the sequence causes the value in AL to be moved to a memory variable. Debug even displays the current contents of that variable (41h). Since in the program, the first statement assigns a value of 10 to X, you can assume that the memory location DS:0260 above is the address of X.

If you continue to step through the next instruction, you will see that the value at DS:0260 is replaced by 0Ah, as shown in Figure 3.8.

```
-t

AX=000A  BX=0000  CX=2D2B  DX=0000  SP=FFEE  BP=0000  SI=0000  DI=0000
DS=738F  ES=738F  SS=738F  CS=738F  IP=2DA8   NV UP EI PL NZ NA PO NC
738F:2DA8 B80500        MOV     AX,0005
-
-d ds:0260
738F:0260  0A 00 B4 06 B0 01 8A 3E-08 00 8A EE 8A 0E 04 00   ..4.0..>...n...
```

Figure 3.8 Single-Stepping through Debug

After executing the next instruction, request a memory dump starting at location DS:0260. The first byte (X) contains 0Ah.

MEMORY ADDRESSING AND SEGMENTATION

The 8088 processor is capable of accessing 1024K bytes of memory. Actually, the PC holds this much memory, although only 640K is available to DOS. Remaining memory is reserved for ROM-BIOS, DOS, display adapters, fixed disk, BASICA, and various device interfaces.

Addressing all this memory requires a special scheme that involves dividing the memory up in blocks of 64K bytes each and generating a 20-bit address, as discussed below.

Memory Addressing

Considering the fact that the 8088 processor has 16-bit registers, you are led to believe that it can only access a maximum of 64K bytes of total memory—the largest 16-bit value; however, you know that this is not true. The PC actually has 1024K bytes of total memory.

The 8088 uses a special technique to address the 1024K bytes of system memory. This technique utilizes a 20-bit address generated by combining a 16-bit address with an offset, as shown here in Figure 3.9.

The 8088 shifts the segment register contents to the left by four bits, in effect multiplying them by 16. To this value, the 8088 adds the offset. The resulting value is the absolute memory address.

Memory Segmentation

Since the 8088 operates on 16-bit quantities, and you have seen that the system memory generates a 20-bit address combining the segment and offset, a special technique is required to allow instructions to build addresses in a program using some type of memory segmentation.

This segmentation is accomplished by splitting the memory up in an arbitrary number of segments, each holding no more than 64K of data, the maximum size addressable by a 16-bit data structure.

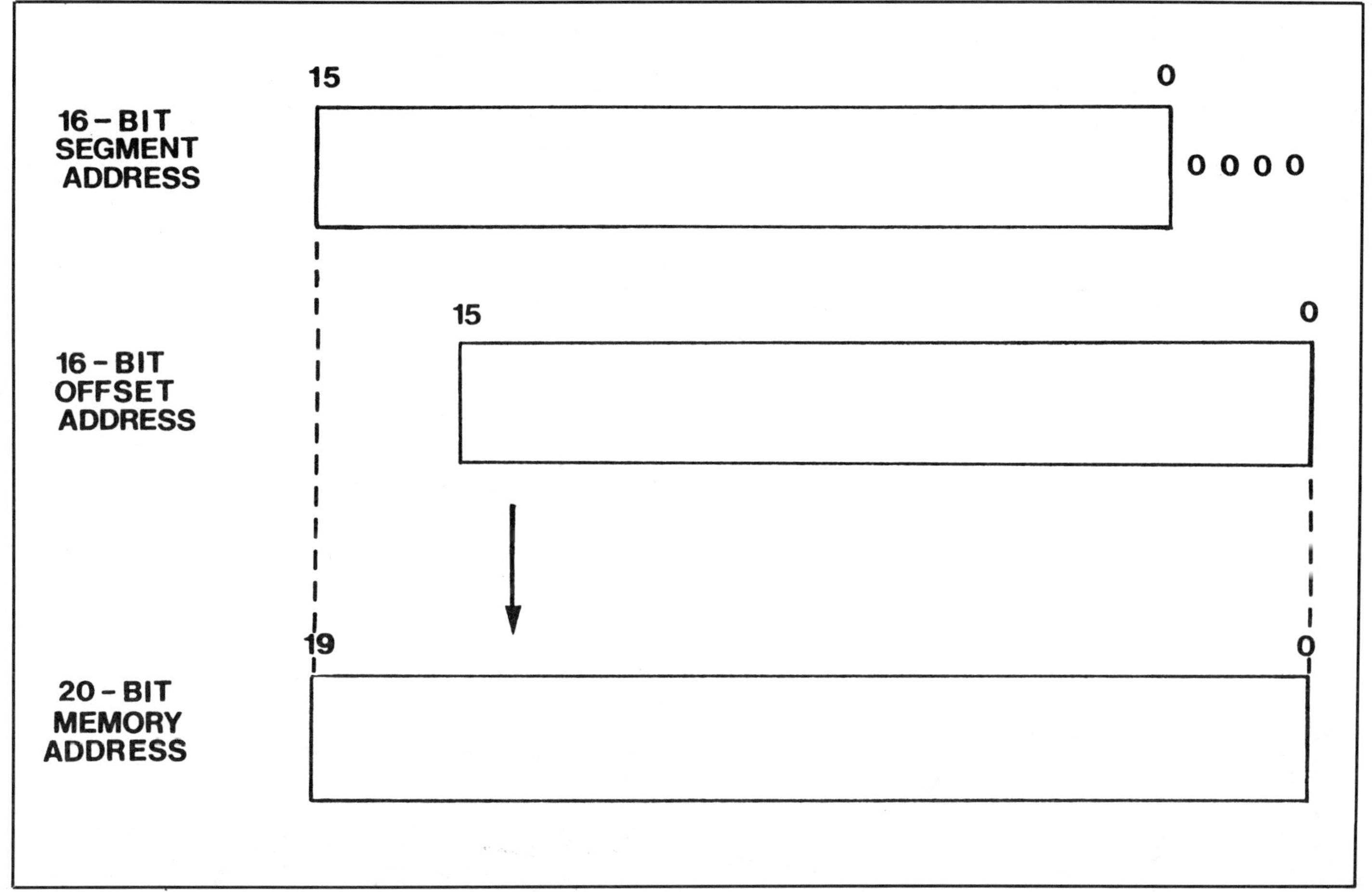

Figure 3.9 Memory Addressing in the 8088

Segments were discussed earlier in the context of registers. Here, think of them as blocks of memory addressable through the segment registers. Specific addresses within each block can be further generated by using index, pointer, and data registers containing the offsets.

Memory Organization of a Turbo Pascal Program

Like any other program, when you load and execute your Turbo Pascal program into memory, the program defines three distinct areas (segments) of memory for its use: the code segment, the data segment, and the stack segment.

The **code segment** primarily contains Turbo's run-time library and the program code. It also contains any typed constants you may have declared in the program. When a program is loaded into memory, the instruction pointer (IP) is automatically set to point to the first instruction in the program. The size of the code segment is 64K bytes, which is also the maximum limit for a program size in the current version (3.01) of Turbo Pascal.

The **data segment** contains the run-time library workspace and global variables (variables declared in the main program block). Like the code segment, the maximum size of the data segment is also 64K.

The **stack segment** contains two principal structures: the **stack** and the **heap.** The stack primarily contains local variables (defined in procedures and functions), parameters (passed by value) and addresses (passed by reference) of parameters passed to subroutines, and intermediate results of expressions. Unlike the other two segments, the maximum size of the stack can be greater than 64K. The stack is maintained by the stack pointer and base pointer registers.

The heap is used to store dynamic variables and is maintained by a special pointer called the **heap pointer**, which is simply an address of the top of the heap, maintained by Turbo's run-time system. This address is updated every time a data element is allocated on the heap.

ADDRESSING I/O PORTS

The 8088 microprocessor communicates with "external" or peripheral devices through input/output ports. You are familiar with the communications port, parallel printer port, and such. All these ports are references to specific I/O port addresses through which the PC can communicate with serial I/O devices such as modems, parallel I/O devices such as Centronics-compatible printers, and so on. There are even specific ports for displaying graphics on the color monitor, reading from and writing to a fixed disk, and adding special interfaces to hook up the PC with laboratory instruments.

The 8088 can access both byte-size ports and word-sized ports. In the 8088, all word-size ports are at odd memory addresses; therefore, they require two accesses by the CPU instead of one for byte-size ports, as you will see later.

Also note that each port has a unique address, and a port may be read only, write only, or both. Because ports are channels to external devices, you must take extra care with the data that comes in and goes out through them.

In later chapters, these I/O ports will be discussed in further detail. You will see how to access them directly in Turbo Pascal or through assembly language routines.

INTERRUPTS

Interrupts are a means of interrupting program execution to perform external tasks, such as communicating with peripherals, updating the system time clock, reporting key pressed condition, etc.

Perhaps the key point to understand about an interrupt on the PC is that it is treated as an asynchronous event, i.e., an event whose timing is unknown. An interrupt can and does occur at any moment during the execution of a program; therefore, the CPU, the operating system, and the program (application) must all be prepared to interrupt current processing and direct attention to the interrupt call.

This type of interruption occurs within a Pascal program when you invoke subprograms—procedures and functions—especially when they are based on certain program conditions. The key difference, however, is that unlike subprograms, which are a part of the main program, the routines executed by the interrupt call are external to the program; therefore, to interrupt program execution and pass control to a sequence of instructions that are outside of the program area, you must take extra precautions and make sure that the control returns to the appropriate instruction in the program without modifying the program environment, which may interfere with further processing.

Because of the way that the interrupt system is implemented in the PC, this facility is already built in to a significant extent. It is further supported by Turbo's **Intr** procedure, as you will see later in this book.

To understand the interrupt handling process, consider a real-life situation in which you are in the middle of reading this chapter and the phone rings. You put the book aside and get up to answer the phone; however, before you put the book aside, you either place a bookmark on the page to indicate where you left off or make a mental note of the paragraph you were reading before you were interrupted. Either of these two actions will ensure that you return to the part where you left off after you have answered the phone call.

In this analogy, reading the book is the active process that is interrupted by the telephone bell (the interrupt). The bookmark records the current position in the process, and answering the phone represents processing the interrupt.

The outcome of interrupt processing is that control is temporarily passed to a specific routine, located outside of the program area (somewhere in high memory), and this routine performs operations for which it is specifically developed.

There are several different types of interrupts on the PC. Their classification is generally based on the context of the discussion. For simplicity, thay are divided into two main categories:

- **hardware interrupts**, generated by external devices requesting attention, such as when a key is pressed
- **software interrupts**, generated by programs requesting specific operating system services (BIOS and DOS routines)

The two interrupt processes are not quite alike, although the manner in which they are processed is very similar. This book primarily focuses on software interrupts.

Interrupt Vectors

Perhaps the most interesting aspect of software interrupts is the way they are processed. The actual routines are mostly located in the ROM, above hex paragraph F000H; however, as far as the applications requesting these services are concerned, these routines can be anywhere in memory. Applications wanting access to specific routines do so indirectly through an 8088 instruction known as the **INT** (**INT**errupt) instruction and an address table located in the lowest 1.5K bytes of memory, starting at absolute address 0H. Since the addresses in this table serve as pointers (or vectors) to other parts of the memory containing the interrupt services, they are frequently referred to as the **interrupt vectors**.

CHAPTER 4

OPERAND ADDRESSING MODES

In previous chapters, while Turbo Pascal programs were traced in Debug, several examples of 8088 instructions were presented. In the process of laying the basic assembly language groundwork, the 8088 processor was also introduced with its general architecture and registers, its memory and I/O port addressing schemes, and its interrupts.

Before the individual instructions in Chapter 5 are covered, one more topic needs attention—the 8088 **Operand Addressing Modes**.

The need for many addressing modes arises from the need to access and operate on different types of operands. As you will discover in the next few chapters, an instruction may operate on several different types of operands, depending on how the operand is addressed and where it is located. The simplest form of operand addressing involves coding operands as part of the instruction. These operands are referred to as **immediate operands**. At the other end of the spectrum, operands may also be addressed using a combination of base register, index register, and displacement. These memory operands are generally part of a complex data structure.

The 8088 processor is able to determine the specific instruction and the operand addressing mode based on the individual bit values coded in the instruction (the machine code value), which will be discussed in detail in Chapter 7 when you learn to convert assembly language into machine code.

This chapter will cover the various operand types and their respective addressing modes.

ADDRESSING MODES

According to Intel's *iAPX 88 Book* (1983), there are 24 unique operand addressing modes. These modes may be grouped by the locations of the operands and the way they are accessed:

1. Direct Addressing

There are several different forms of direct addressing modes:

- **Immediate**—operand is part of the instruction, following the one-byte instruction op (operation) code

- **Register**—operand is in a register
- **Direct**—operand is memory-based and the instruction contains its address offset
- **Register Indirect**—a register is used as a pointer to access the operand, i.e., it holds the memory address of the operand

2. Base or Index Register + Displacement

Contents of index or base register are added to the one or two-byte data (displacement) contained in the instruction to access the operand address.

3. Base Register + Index + Displacement

Contents of index and base registers are added to the one or two-byte data (displacement) in the instruction to access the operand address.

In each mode, the objective is to generate the **Effective Address (EA)** of the operand to be accessed. The EA is added to the segment address to get the absolute address.

The more complex addressing modes may appear analogous to the way you access data structures in Pascal. For example, individual elements in an array are accessed by specifying the base address of the array and an indexing value relative to the position of the specific element. With more complex data structures, such as arrays within records, the addressing scheme similarly becomes more complicated. Keeping this in mind, you can begin to appreciate the 24 possible addressing modes for operands in assembly language instructions.

REVIEWING THE 8088 ADDRESSING REGISTERS

Before proceeding with the various addressing modes of the 8088, first review the addressing registers as discussed in Chapter 3.

The four registers that participate in operand addressing modes are BX, BP, SI, and DI. You may recall that BX is one of the four general-purpose registers. It is used as a base register in addressing modes, which will be explained later in this chapter. The Base Pointer register is often used in programs to access specific data items from the stack. The two index registers—Source Index and Destination Index—are used in many string manipulation instructions as well as in accessing specific items in complex data structures.

Note that programs may only access these registers as 16-bit data structures, unlike the general-purpose registers, which are accessible as 8 and 16-bit entities.

In addition to the above roles, these registers are also used in several different combinations to generate the operand address.

FOUR-COMPONENT ADDRESSING

Earlier in this chapter, several "quantities" were mentioned, such as base address, index, and displacement, which are used to generate the actual operand address.

In the most complex operand addressing scheme, four components are used to refer to an operand in an instruction:

- **Segment Address**—the starting address of the segment in which the operand is located. This address is stored in one of the four segment registers (CS, DS, SS, and ES). Since you most frequently access operands in the data segment, this segment address is generally contained in the DS register.

- **Base Address**—generally the starting address of the data structure in which the operand is located. For example, the address of the first element of an array or table may be used as a base address to calculate the address of the "nth" element. Registers BX and BP are mostly used to store the base address of an operand.

- **Index**—used frequently when you are accessing structures within structures. The index is used in conjunction with the base address or displacement or both. Registers SI and DI are used to store indexing values.

Displacement—a fixed value specified in the instruction that is added to the base address (contained in the base or segment register) or indexing value to calculate the operand address. Displacement may be 8 or 16-bit, depending on the size of the structure in which the operand is located.

Note that because displacement is part of the instruction, it is a **static** (fixed) value, whereas the base address and index are **dynamic** (variant) values since they may be altered during program execution.

DIRECT ADDRESSING MODE

Direct operand addressing is the simplest form of specifying the operand address in an instruction. As stated earlier, there are several different forms of direct addressing modes.

Immediate Addressing

Immediate addressing refers to situations where the operand in consideration is specified in the instruction itself, i.e., it is a part of the instruction, following the one-byte instruction op (operation) code.

For example:

```
mov ah,1Ah
add dx,13h
```

In these instructions, 1Ah and 13h are referred to as immediate operands since they are specified in the instructions. The operand may be byte or word-sized.

These instructions are analogous to the following assignment statements in Turbo Pascal:

```
x := 100;
Count := 0;
```

Register

In the register addressing mode, the operand is accessed from or stored in a register. For example:

```
mov ax,dx
inc cx
```

In the first example, the value in register dx is copied into the accumulator. In the second example, the operand is in register cx and is incremented by one.

Direct

In the direct addressing mode, the operand is in memory, and its offset is specified in the instruction in the form of displacement (from the segment register). This displacement (or **effective address**) is added to the segment register to calculate the 20-bit absolute memory address.

For example:

```
mov ax,[260]
inc [80]
```

The operand enclosed in square brackets is treated as the displacement of the operand from the current data segment. The actual value at that location is copied into the ax register in the first example and incremented by one in the second example.

As you saw in earlier examples in the book, the immediate assignment statement in Turbo Pascal translates into two assembly language statements, as shown here:

Turbo Pascal:

```
X := 10;
```

Assembly Language:

```
mov   ax,10
mov   [260],ax
```

The actual displacement in the second statement will vary depending on the location of x in the data segment.

Register Indirect

In the register indirect form of addressing, the address offset of the operand is specified in a register. Following that specification, the instruction accessing that operand will obtain the offset from the register and add it to the segment address (contained in a segment register) to get the operand address.

For example:

```
mov ax,[bx]
inc [bp]
```

In the first example, the data at the address specified by the BX register is copied into the accumulator. In the second example, the data at the address specified in the BP register is incremented by one.

Note that in these instructions, the contents of the registers are simply addresses of actual data items; therefore values in registers are not altered as a result of the operation. Here, registers behave as pointers.

BASE OR INDEX REGISTER + DISPLACEMENT

In this group, there are two very similar addressing modes, differing only in the register (base or index) used in the relative addressing scheme.

Base + Displacement

In Base + Displacement addressing mode, the **effective address (EA)** of the operand is calculated by adding the displacement to the contents of the base register. Here again, the displacement is part of the instruction. The base registers are BX and BP.

For example:

```
mov   ax,[bx]+260
inc   byte ptr [bx + 260]
```

You will see several ways of expressing these instructions, as shown here:

```
inc byte ptr [bx] + 260
inc byte ptr [bx] [260]
inc byte ptr [bx] + [260]
inc byte ptr [bx] + 260
```

All forms are interpreted the same way, i.e., the displacement is added to the contents of the bx register to calculate the effective address, which is the offset from the current data segment.

Index + Displacement

In Index + Displacement addressing mode, the effective address of the operand is calculated by adding the displacement to the contents of the index register. Here again, the displacement is part of the instruction. The index registers are SI and DI.

For example:

```
mov   ax,[di]+260
inc   byte ptr [di + 260]
```

BASE REGISTER + INDEX + DISPLACEMENT

When accessing complex structures, such as tables and records, you need more than a base address and displacement to get the effective address of an operand. The Base + Index + Displacement mode allows you to use all three elements (base register, index register, and displacement) in the scheme to get the effective address of an operand.

For example:

```
mov ax,[bx] + [di] + 260
```

This instruction will generate the effective address of the operand by adding together the displacement and the contents of bx and di registers.

In the next two chapters, instructions of the 8088 will be briefly discussed. These discussions are designed to serve both as tutorials and reference.

CHAPTER 5

THE INSTRUCTION SET

In Chapters 1, 2, and 3, you looked at several examples of simple Turbo Pascal programs in Debug. The idea was to become familiar with Debug's environment, as well as learn about the 8088's architecture, registers, and memory addressing schemes.

Now you can begin to look at the assembly language instructions that are the core of a program. These instructions control a program's operations, i.e., what it does and how.

This chapter begins with a discussion of the 8088 instruction set. There are over 90 instructions in the set, and they perform a wide variety of operations, from data transfer and simple arithmetic to communication with input/output devices. For the purpose of ordering them in some logical manner, these instructions have been grouped by their generic functions. For example, an instruction that transfers data from a register to the stack (PUSH) and one that transfers data from a register to a memory location (MOV) are considered to be in the same group (Data Transfer Instructions) although they are used for different purposes. The objective in this chapter is to present them in a format that is suitable for reference as well as tutorial purposes. Included here are instructions that are commonly used and brief descriptions of them. The main emphasis is on their use in Turbo Pascal programs.

This chapter and Chapter 6 will cover the instruction set. This chapter is divided into the following major groups:

- Data transfer instructions
- Arithmetic instructions
- Logical instructions

DATA TRANSFER INSTRUCTIONS

This group of instructions is used to move data items. Moving, transferring, or, more appropriately, copying of data may occur as follows:

- From memory location to register
- From register to memory location
- Between register and I/O port
- Between registers

The data item may be a value or an address of a value.

The following instructions in this group are addressed here:

MOV	moves byte or word between register and memory
PUSH	moves word from register or memory to stack
POP	moves word from stack to register or memory
XCHG	exchanges byte or word between two locations
XLAT	moves corresponding byte from table into AL
IN	moves byte or word from input port to register
OUT	moves byte or word from register to output port
LEA	loads offset address of memory operand into register
LDS	loads double word from memory into any register + DS
LES	loads double word from memory into any register + ES

General Data Transfer

The MOV instruction is commonly used to transfer byte and word-size data items between operands. XCHG allows you to swap two variables in a single instruction.

Move Data (MOV)
Flags Affected: none

The **MOV** instruction is used to transfer a byte or word of data from a source, which may be a register or a memory location, to a destination, which may be a memory location or a register.

Depending on the source and operands, as well as various addressing modes, there are several different versions of the MOV instruction. You will look at examples of each one of its forms. Table 5.1 lists the different ways in which MOV can be used to move data from a source to a destination; an example for each condition follows.

Table 5.1

SOURCE		DESTINATION	EXAMPLE	
Memory	→	Accumulator	mov	ax,file_size
Accumulator	→	Memory	mov	page,ax
Register	→	Register	mov	ax,bx
Register	→	Memory	mov	bios_data,bx
Memory	→	Register	mov	ax,io_char
Immediate	→	Register	mov	ah,0Fh
Immediate	→	Memory	mov	displ_attr,12
Register	→	Segment-Register	mov	ds,bx
Memory	→	Segment-Register	mov	ds,screen_base
Segment-Reg	→	Register	mov	ax,ds
Segment-Reg	→	Memory	mov	seg_ptr,ds

Here are some more common examples of MOV:

```
mov ah,9h
mov word ptr [bx],8000h
mov file_size,ax
mov dx,[bx]
mov al,dl
mov ax,cs:init_val
mov ds:file_int,ax
```

MOV is one of the most commonly used instructions in assembly language for two good reasons. First, most instructions require that at least one of their operands be in a register; therefore, you will use MOV to move that operand into the specified register before executing an instruction. Second, operations involving registers are considerably faster than those that require the processor to fetch data from external memory; therefore, for speed and efficiency, programmers frequently move data into a register before performing operations on it.

Restrictions on MOV

There are a few restrictions that apply to MOV (see Table 5.1).

First, note that MOV cannot perform data transfer between two memory locations. For you to move data between two memory locations, you first must move it from a memory location (source) into a general-purpose register and then from that register to the second memory location (destination).

Example:

```
mov ax,scr_attr
mov attr_char,ax
```

Second, MOV cannot be used to transfer data from one segment register to another. This operation requires two steps: first, move the value from the source segment register into a general-purpose register; then, move it from the general purpose register to the destination segment register.

Example:

```
mov ax,ds
mov es,ax
```

Finally, MOV cannot be used to load an immediate value into a segment register. Again, a value should first be loaded (or moved) into a general-purpose register before it is moved into a segment register.

Example:

```
mov ax,b800h
mov es,ax
```

Exchange (XCHG)
Flags Affected: none

While MOV actually copies the contents of source to destination, the **XCHG** instruction exchanges the contents of source and destination operands.

There are several versions of the XCHG instruction, depending on the operands. Table 5.2 lists the possible combinations. Furthermore, the XCHG instruction can be used to exchange either a byte or word value between two operands.

Table 5.2

SOURCE		DESTINATION	EXAMPLE
Memory	↔	Register	xchg ax,file_size
Register	↔	Register	xchg cx,dx
Register	↔	Accumulator	xchg ax,cx

Following are some more common examples of XCHG:

```
xchg bl,bh
xchg si,cx
xchg buf_size,ax
```

Exchanging the contents of two operands without this instruction would involve three steps and a possible third operand. There are two ways to perform this exchange:

1. Using MOV and the last example:

```
mov cx,ax
mov ax,buf_size
mov buf_size,cx
```

   Here, you use the CX register as a temporary location for storing the value of AX.

2. Using XOR's:

```
xor ax,buf_size
xor buf_size,ax
xor ax,buf_size
```

   Using XOR's works more efficiently and without a third variable. The XOR instruction has not been covered yet. For more details on the mechanism of XOR's, see XOR later in this chapter.

The above steps show you the usefulness of XCHG and also alternatives to XCHG in situations where XCHG does not work.

I/O Instructions

The 8088 uses two instructions—IN and OUT—to read from and write to various I/O ports.

Reading In (IN)
Flags Affected: none

The **IN** instruction reads in data from an I/O port to the accumulator. It reads a byte of data if the destination operand is specified as AL and a word if the destination is AX. The address of the port to be read from may be specified as an immediate operand or placed in the DX register. The immediate operand allows access to ports numbered 0 through 255. By placing the value in DX, ports numbered 0 through 65,535 can be accessed.

Example:

```
mov dx,03DAh
in  al,dx
```

Writing Out (OUT)
Flags Affected: none

The **OUT** instruction writes out data to an I/O port from the accumulator. It reads a byte of data if the source operand is specified as AL and a word if the source operand is AX. The address of the port to be written to may be specified as an immediate operand or placed in the DX register. The immediate operand allows access to ports numbered 0 through 255. By placing the value in DX, ports numbered 0 through 65,535 can be accessed.

Example:

```
out 43h,al
mov dx,20h
out dx,al
```

Stack Manipulation Instructions

The stack structure was discussed in Chapters 2 and 3. A few instructions allow you to store ("push") data onto the stack and retrieve ("pop") data from the stack.

Pushing onto the Stack (PUSH)
Flags Affected: none

PUSH transfers a word of data from the source operand to the top of the stack. The stack pointer register, which monitors the stack, is automatically incremented by two. PUSH is frequently used to place data temporarily onto the stack. It is also used to pass parameters to subroutines.

The operand for PUSH may be a register, a segment register (except CS), and a memory location.

Example:

```
push ds
push si
```

Popping from the Stack (POP)
Flags Affected: none

POP transfers a word of data from the top of the stack to the source operand. The stack pointer register, which monitors the stack, is automatically decremented by two. POP is used to retrieve data temporarily saved on the stack by PUSH It is also used to retrieve parameters passed to subroutines.

The operand for POP may be a register, a segment register (except CS), and a memory location.

Example:

```
pop ds
pop si
```

Table Lookup and Translation

The single instruction XLAT allows you to look up tables and perform conversions quickly and efficiently.

Translate (XLAT)
Flags Affected: none

The **XLAT** instruction works with user-defined translate tables. It replaces a byte in the accumulator (AL) with a corresponding byte from the translate table. The address of the table must have been previously placed in BX.

XLAT uses the value in AL as an offset to the table that begins at the address in BX.

Example:

```
mov al,5
mov bx, offset table
xlat table
```

In this example, the fifth element in the table will be moved into AL as a result of XLAT.

XLAT is used commonly for translating character sets from one format to another, for example, from ASCII to IBM's EBCDIC and vice versa.

Address Transfers

So far, you have looked at instructions that transfer data between operands. In contrast, LEA, LDS, and LES are instructions that transfer addresses of data items rather than their contents. These addresses serve as pointers to the data items. The 16-bit offset address is loaded into the specified register, and the segment address is loaded into either the DS (LDS) or the ES (LES) register.

Load Effective Address (LEA)
Flags Affected: none

LEA transfers the offset address of its memory operand into the specified general, pointer, or index register.

Example:

```
lea di,[bx+2]
lea dx,buffer
lea ax,table
```

Load Pointer Using DS (LDS) or ES (LES)
Flags Affected: none

The **LDS** and **LES** instructions work the same way as LEA described above with an additional feature being that the segment address is loaded into the DS register (LDS) or the ES register (LES).

Example:

```
lds bx,buff_ptr
```

In addition to the instructions discussed above, there are several other data transfer instructions that have been grouped with the string instructions. These instructions will be covered later in this chapter.

ARITHMETIC INSTRUCTIONS

The 8088 instruction set contains a fairly large collection of instructions that allow you to perform addition, subtraction, multiplication, and division on a wide variety of numeric data formats such as signed, unsigned, BCD, and ASCII.

The following instructions will be discussed in this section:

ADD	Addition
ADC	Add with carry
INC	Increment
AAA	ASCII adjust for addition
DAA	Decimal adjust for addition
UB	Subtraction
SBB	Subtract with borrow
DEC	Decrement
NEG	Negate byte or word
AAS	ASCII adjust for subtraction
DAS	Decimal adjust for subtraction
MUL	Multiplication
IMUL	Interger multiplication
AAM	ASCII adjust for multiply
DIV	Division
IDIV	Integer division
AAD	ASCII adjust for division
CBW	Convert byte to word
CWD	Convert word to double word

Addition Instructions

These instructions—ADD, ADC, INC, AAA, and DAA—perform addition on a variety of data formats—the accumulator, data register, or memory operand.

Add (ADD) and Add with Carry (ADC)
Flags Affected: AF, CF, OF, PF, SF, ZF

Both the **ADD** and **ADC** instructions add their two operands, placing the resulting sum in the destination operand. They operate on byte and word-size values. The operands may be signed or unsigned binary numbers. ADC incorporates a carry from a previous operation if the carry flag (CF) was set during the previous add; therefore, the ADC can be used to add numbers longer than 16 bits.

ADD and ADC work on a variety of operands. Table 5.3 lists the various possibilities with examples.

Table 5.3

SOURCE		DESTINATION	EXAMPLE
Register	→	Register	adc ax,cx
Register	→	Memory	add linect,bx
Memory	→	Register	add ax,count
Immediate	→	Register	adc bl,0Fh
Immediate	→	Memory	add counter,12h
Immediate	→	Accumulator	add al,040h

As is evident in Table 5.3, certain restrictions on operands apply to both ADD and ADC. For example, you cannot add two memory operands directly. One of them must be moved into one of the general-purpose registers.

Increment (INC)
Flags Affected: AF, OF, PF, SF, ZF

The **INC** instruction increments its operand by one. The operand may be byte or word-sized and an 8-bit or 16-bit register or memory operand.

Example:

```
inc ax
inc count
```

ASCII Adjust for Addition (AAA)
Flags Affected: AF, CF, OF, PF, XF, ZF

You can use the addition instructions just described to perform addition on numbers stored or expressed in the ASCII format, which saves you the extra step of converting the formats for each operand before performing the operation; however, the result should be converted to a decimal number. The **AAA** instruction automatically performs the conversion. The only catch is that the operand must be in the AL register; therefore, AAA should be used immediately after an addition in which AL is the destination operand.

Example:

```
add al,bl
aaa
```

Decimal Adjust for Addition (DAA)
Flags Affected: AF, CF, PF, XF, ZF

Similar to AAA, you can use the addition instructions described above to perform addition on numbers stored or expressed in the BCD (packed decimal) format, which saves you the extra step of converting the formats for each operand before performing the operation; however, the result should be converted to a packed decimal number. The **DAA** instruction automatically performs the conversion. The only catch is that the operand must be in the AL register; therefore, DAA should be used immediately after an addition in which AL is the destination operand.

Example:

```
add al,bl
daa
```

The contents of the two operands to be added prior to DAA should be in packed decimal format, and the AL register should be the destination operand.

Subtraction Instructions

These instructions—SUB, SBB, DEC, AAS, DAS, and NEG—perform subtraction on a variety of data formats—the accumulator, data register, or memory operand.

Subtract (SUB) and Subtract with Borrow (SBB)
Flags Affected: AF, CF, OF, PF, SF, ZF

Both the **SUB** and **SBB** instructions subtract the source from the destination operand, placing the resulting difference in the destination operand. They operate on byte and word-size values. The operands may be signed or unsigned binary numbers. SBB deducts one from the result if the carry flag (CF) was set during the previous subtract; therefore, SSB can be used to subtract numbers longer than 16 bits.

SUB and SBB work on a variety of operands. Table 5.4 lists the various possibilities with examples.

Table 5.4

SOURCE		DESTINATION	EXAMPLE
Register	→	Register	sub ax,cx
Register	→	Memory	sub linect,bx
Memory	→	Register	sub ax,count
Immediate	→	Register	sbb bl,0Fh
Immediate	→	Memory	sub counter,12h
Immediate	→	Accumulator	sub al,040h

As is evident in Table 5.4, certain restrictions on operands apply to both SUB and SBB. For example, you cannot perform subtraction directly on two memory operands. One of them must be moved into one of the general-purpose registers.

Decrement (DEC)
Flags Affected: AF, OF, PF, SF, ZF

DEC instruction decrements its operand by one. The operand may be byte or word-sized and an 8-bit or 16-bit register or memory operand.

Example:

```
dec ax
dec count
```

ASCII Adjust for Subtraction (ASS)
Flags Affected: AF, CF, OF, PF, XF, ZF

You can use the subtraction instructions just described to perform subtraction on numbers stored or expressed in the ASCII format, which saves you the extra step of converting the formats for each operand before performing the operation; however, the result should be converted to a decimal number. The **AAS** instruction automatically performs the conversion. The only catch is that the operand must be in the AL register; therefore, SUB should be used immediately after an addition in which AL is the destination operand.

Example:

```
sub al,bl
aas
```

Decimal Adjust for Subtraction (DAS)
Flags Affected: AF, CF, PF, XF, ZF

Similar to DAA, you can use the subtraction instructions described above to perform subtraction on numbers stored or expressed in the BCD (packed decimal) format, which saves you the extra step of converting the formats for each operand before performing the operation; however, the result should be converted to a packed decimal number. The **DAS** instruction automatically performs the conversion. The only catch is that the operand must be in the AL register; therefore, DAS should be used immediately after an addition in which AL is the destination operand.

Example:

```
sub al,bl
das
```

The contents of the two operands used in the subtraction prior to DAS should be in packed decimal format, and the AL register should be the destination operand.

Negate (NEG)
Flags Affected: AF, CF, OF, PF, SF, ZF

The **NEG** instruction negates the operand, thereby converting the operand into its two's complement form. NEG operates on both byte and word-sized operands.

For a discussion of two's complement, refer to Chapter 1.

Negate can operate on registers as well as on operands in memory. The instruction actually causes the operand to be subtracted from zero, thereby negating its value.

Example:

```
neg al
neg
```

Multiplication Instructions

These instructions—MUL, IMUL, and AAM—perform multiplication on a variety of data formats—the accumulator, data register, or memory operand.

Multiply (MUL) and Integer Multiply (IMUL)
Flags Affected: AF, CF, OF, PF, SF, ZF

Both the **MUL** and **IMUL** instructions multiply their two operands, placing the result in the destination operand, which is always the accumulator. They operate on byte and word-sized values. When using an 8-bit value as source, the instruction multiplies the value by AL, and the result is returned in AH-AL. When the source operand is a 16-bit value, the result is returned in DX-AX register pair. Flags CF and OF are set if the DX or AH registers contain significant digits of the result.

The operands may be unsigned (MUL) or signed (IMUL) binary numbers.

Both MUL and IMUL work on a variety of source operand types. Table 5.5 lists the various possibilities with examples. Remember that the destination is always AL or AX, depending on the size of the source operand.

Table 5-5

SOURCE	EXAMPLE
Register (8-bit)	mul bh
Register (16-bit)	imul cx
Memory (8-bit)	mul pos_byte
Memory (16-bit)	mul pos_word

As is evident from Table 5.5, certain restrictions on operands apply to both MUL and IMUL. For example, you cannot use an immediate operand in multiplication operations. The operand must be moved into one of the general-purpose registers.

ASCII Adjust for Multiply (AAM)
Flags Affected: PF, SF, ZF

You can use the multiplication instructions just described to perform multiplication on numbers stored or expressed in the unpacked BCD (ASCII) format, which saves you the extra step of converting the formats for each operand before performing the operation; however, the result should be converted to an unpacked decimal number. The **AAM** instruction automatically performs the conversion.

Example:

```
mul bl
aam
```

The result of this instruction is a valid, 2-digit, unpacked number in the AH-AL register pair.

Division Instructions

These instructions—DIV, IDIV, and AAD—perform division on a variety of data formats—the accumulator, data register, or memory operand.

In addition, two instructions—CBW and CWD—are used to expand the operand size to a word from a byte and a double word from a word respectively for adjusting the size of an operand for division.

Division (DIV) and Integer Division (IDIV)
Flags Affected: undefined

Both the **DIV** and **IDIV** instructions perform division on their two operands, placing the result in the destination operand, which is always the accumulator. They operate on byte and word-size values. When the instructions use an 8-bit value as source, the dividend is a 16-bit value in AX, and the result is returned in AL (quotient) and AH (remainder). When the source operand is a 16-bit value, the dividend is 32 bits wide in the DX-AX register pair, and the result is returned in AX (quotient) and DX (remainder) register pair.

Flags are left undefined as a result of these two instructions.

The operands may be unsigned (MUL) or signed (IMUL) binary numbers.

Both MUL and IMUL work on a variety of source operand types. Table 5.6 lists the various possibilities with examples. Remember that the destination is always AX, depending on the size of the source operand.

Table 5.6

SOURCE	EXAMPLE
Register (8-bit)	div bh
Register (16-bit)	idiv cx
Memory (8-bit)	div pos__byte
Memory (16-bit)	div pos__word

As is evident in Table 5.6, certain restrictions on operands apply to both DIV and IDIV. For example, you cannot use an immediate operand in division operations. The operand must be moved into one of the general-purpose registers.

ASCII Adjust for Division (AAD)
Flags Affected: PF, SF, ZF

AAM modifies the number in AL before performing the division, which is different from the other ASCII adjust instructions that perform the conversion after the arithmetic operation. As a result of the division, the quotient is a valid, unpacked decimal (ASCII) number. The instruction only applies to division involving an 8-bit source operand, i.e., AH = 0, before the division operation.

Example:

```
aad
div bl
```

The result of this instruction is one valid, unpacked digit each for quotient (AL) and remainder (AL).

Convert Byte to Word (CBW)
Flags Affected: none

The division instructions discussed earlier require a word or double word-sized operand as the divisor. If you are faced with an 8-bit value in AL and are attempting to divide with an 8-bit value in the source operand, you must first "expand" the value into AH without altering it. This expansion simply requires extending the sign of the value into the AH register.

The **CBW** instruction extends the sign of a value in AL to the AH register so that it becomes a 16-bit data item. The actual operation simply involves filling up the AH register with zeroes for positive numbers and ones for negative numbers.

Example:

```
mov bh,4
mov al,01Fh
cbw
div bh
```

Convert Word to Double Word
Flags Affected: none

Similar to CBW above, if you are faced with a 16-bit value in AX and are attempting to divide it with another 16-bit value in the source operand, you must first "expand" the value into DX without altering it. This expansion simply requires extending the sign of the value into the DX register.

The **CWD** instruction extends the sign of a value in AX to the DX register so that it becomes a 32-bit data item. The actual operation simply involves filling up the DX register with zeroes for positive numbers and ones for negative numbers.

Example:

```
mov bx,02ADh
mov ax,FFCAh
cwd
div bx
```

LOGICAL INSTRUCTIONS

The 8088 instruction set consists of several instructions that perform Boolean, bit-shifting, and bit-rotating operations. All of these instructions are grouped as logical instructions.

These instructions are further grouped into three subtypes:

- Boolean instructions—AND, OR, XOR, NOT, TEST
- Bit-shifting instructions—SHL, SHR, SAL, SAR
- Bit-rotating instructions—ROL ROR, RCL, RCR

These groups will be discussed briefly in this section.

Boolean Instructions

These instructions perform Boolean operations (AND, OR, XOR, NOT) between operands. The TEST instruction performs the same function as AND, except the operands remain unaltered.

Logical AND (AND)
Flags Affected: CF, OF, PF, SF, ZF

The **AND** instruction performs the logical "AND" between its operands and returns the result of the operation in the destination operand.

Logical AND results in a bit being set (to a 1) if and only if the corresponding bits in both operands are set; otherwise, it is cleared (set to 0).

AND is often used to selectively turn "OFF" bits in an operand (a memory operand or register).

To understand the way the logical AND works, look at the following examples:

Example 1:

```
        A = 00100111   27H
        B = 11111110   FEH
            --------   ---
  A AND B = 00100110   26H
            --------   ---
```

Example 2:

```
        A = 11110110   F6H
        B = 00001111   0FH
            --------   ---
  A AND B = 00000110   06H
            --------   ---
```

As a result of "ANDing" A with B in Example 1, bit 0 of A is turned off; therefore, its value is altered to 26H.

Similarly, as a result of ANDing A with B in Example 2, the four most significant bits of A are turned off; therefore, its value is altered to 06.

Logical AND (TEST)
Flags Affected: CF, OF, PF, SF, ZF

The **TEST** instruction performs the logical AND between its operands and sets the flag, but the operands remain unaltered as a result of the operation.

TEST is often used in conjunction with Jump instructions. For example:

```
test AL,8
jnz  PROCESS
```

This instruction will perform a logical AND between the AL register and immediate operand 08H. In effect, this process is the same as checking to see if bit 3 is set to a 1. If it is set to a 1, then the jump occurs; otherwise, the instruction following the jnz is executed.

Logical OR (OR)
Flags Affected: CF, OF, PF, SF, ZF

The **OR** instruction performs the logical "OR" between its operands, and returns the result of the operation in the destination operand.

Logical OR results in a bit being set (to a 1) if the corresponding bit in either (or both) of the operands is set; otherwise, it is cleared (set to 0).

OR is often used to selectively turn "ON" bits in an operand (a memory operand or register).

To understand the way the logical OR works, look at the following examples:

Example 1:

```
     A = 00100111   27H
     B = 11111110   FEH
         --------   ---
A OR B = 11111111   FFH
         --------   ---
```

Example 2:

```
     A = 00000110   06H
     B = 11110000   F0H
         --------   ---
A OR B = 11110110   F6H
         --------   ---
```

As a result of "ORing" A with B in Example 1, bits 3, 4, 6, and 7 of operand A are turned "ON"; therefore, its value is altered to FFH.

Similarly, as a result of "ORing" A with B in Example 2, the four most significant bits of A are turned "ON"; therefore, its value is altered to F6H.

Logical eXclusive OR (XOR)
Flags Affected: CF, OF, PF, SF, ZF

The **XOR** instruction performs the logical "eXclusive OR" between its operands and returns the result of the operation in the destination operand.

Logical XOR results in a bit being set (to a 1) if the corresponding bit in either *but not both* of the operands is set; otherwise, it is cleared (set to 0).

To understand the way the logical "eXclusive OR" works, look at the following examples:

Example 1:

```
        A = 00100111   27H
        B = 11111110   FEH
            --------   ---
  A XOR B = 11011001   D9H
            --------   ---
```

Example 2:

```
        A = 00000110   06H
        B = 11110000   F0H
            --------   ---
   A OR B = 11110110   F6H
            --------   ---
```

As a result of "eXclusive ORing" A with B in Example 1, bits 1, 2, and 5 are turned "OFF," and 3, 4, 6, and 7 of operand A are turned "ON"; therefore, its value is altered to D9H.

Similarly, as a result of "eXclusive ORing" A with B in Example 2, the four most significant bits of A are turned "ON"; therefore, its value is altered to F6H.

The XOR operator is frequently used to swap the values of two operands, quite like the XCHG instruction.

If you look at the values of A and B before and after three XOR's are performed, you will realize that they have been swapped.

```
A = 10001110            B = 11001100

Step 1   A XOR B

               A = 10001110
               B = 11001100
                   --------
A = (A XOR B)      01000010
                   --------

Step 2.  B XOR A

               B = 11001100
               A = 01000010
                   --------
B = (B XOR A)      10001110
                   --------

Step 3.  A XOR B
               B = 10001110
               A = 01000010
                   --------
A = (A XOR B)      11001100
                   --------

A = 11001100            B = 10001110
```

XOR is also commonly used to clear out an operand, as shown here:

```
               A = 10001110
               A = 10001110
                   --------
A = (A XOR A)      00000000
                   --------
```

Logical NOT (NOT)
Flags Affected: none

The **NOT** instruction complements its operand.

Logical NOT results in the "inversion" of bits, i.e., a bit that was set to a 1 is cleared and vice versa.

To understand the way that this bit complementing works, look at the following examples:

```
A = 00000000              not A = 11111111
A = 00010101              not A = 11101010
```

Bit-Shifting Instructions

These instructions perform bit logical (SHL, SHR) and arithmetic (SAL, SAR) shifting of bits in the operand.

Shift Logical Left (SHL) and Shift Arthmetic Left (SAL)
Flags Affected: CF, OF, PF, SF, ZF

These instructions shift bits in the destination operand to the left by the number specified in the immediate operand (which can only be 1) or in the counter (CL register).

Example 1:

```
      A = 00000101
A shl 1 = 00001010  <— 0
A shl 3 = 00101000  <— 000
```

During this shift, the leftmost bits are shifted out and passed through the CF flag. "0" bits fill up the rightmost position.

Left shifting of bits is equivalent to multiplying the operand by two with each shift. Shifting, like other bit operations, is considerably faster than arithmetic operations such as multiplication.

Shift Logical Right (SHR)
Flags Affected: CF, OF, PF, SF, ZF

This instruction shifts bits in the destinat on operand to the right by the number specified in the immediate operand (which can only be 1) or in the counter (CL register).

Example 1:

```
        A = 00000101
  A shr 1 = 00000010   —> 0
  A shr 3 = 00000000   —> 000
```

During this shift, the rightmost bits are shifted out and passed through the CF flag. "0" bits fill up the leftmost position.

Shift Arithmetic Right (SAR)
Flags Affected: CF, OF, PF, SF, ZF

This instruction shifts bits in the destination operand to the right by the number specified in the immediate operand (1) or in the counter (CL register). It differs from SHR in that the sign bit is preserved.

Bit-Rotating Instructions

These instructions perform bit rotation to the left (ROL, RCL) or right (ROR, RCR).

Rotate Right (ROR)
Flags Affected: CF, OF

This instruction rotates bits in the destination operand to the right by the number specified in the immediate operand (1) or in the Counter Register (CL).

Example 1:

```
      A = 00000101
A ror 1 = 10000010
A ror 3 = 10100000
```

Rotate Left (ROL)
Flags Affected: CF, OF

This instruction rotates bits in the destination operand to the left by the number specified in the immediate operand (1) or in the Counter Register (CL).

Example 1:

```
      A = 10000101
A rol 1 = 00001011
A rol 3 = 00101100
```

Rotate Through Carry Right (RCR)
Flags Affected: CF, OF

This instruction is similar to ROR, except that the Carry Flag (CF) becomes the leftmost bit of the destination operand, and the bits move through the flag. Conversely, as a result of the rotation, its bit also moves into the high-order position of the destination operand.

Rotate Through Carry Left (RCL)
Flags Affected: CF, OF

This instruction is similar to ROL, except that the Carry Flag (CF) becomes the rightmost bit of the destination operand, and the bits move through the flag. Conversely, as a result of the rotation, its bit also moves into the low-order position of the destination operand.

CHAPTER 6

THE INSTRUCTION SET PART II

In Chapter 5, some of the 8088 instructions were discussed. These instructions were grouped into several functional groups, and you examined the first few groups, which emphasized the more frequently encountered instructions.

In this chapter, coverage of the 8088 instruction set is concluded. The following groups are covered:

- Compare instruction
- Jump instructions
- Subroutine-handling instructions
- Loop instructions
- String instructions
- Flag instructions
- Interrupt instructions

COMPARE INSTRUCTION

A single instruction (CMP) in this category is used to compare two 8-bit or 16-bit data items.

Compare Data (CMP)
Flags Affected: AF, CF, OF, PF, SF, ZF

The compare instruction, often grouped with arithmetic instructions, performs a subtraction on two 8-bit or 16-bit numbers. Instead of returning the results, it updates the flag based on the result of the subtraction. The subtraction process is performed using two's complement arithmetic.

Note that CMP does not alter the contents of the operands. The flags are updated based on how the destination compares to the source.

Depending on the source and destination operands, there are several different versions of the CMP instruction. You will look at examples of each one of its forms. Table 6.1 lists the different ways in which CMP can be used to compare two operands.

Table 6.1

SOURCE		DESTINATION	EXAMPLE
Register	→	Register	cmp dx,di
Register	→	Memory	cmp count,cx
Memory	→	Register	cmp dx,sum
Immediate	→	Register	cmp cx,FFFFh
Immediate	→	Memory	cmp attr,7
Immediate	→	Accumulator	cmp ax,10h

CMP is most commonly used in **conditional branching logic** where the branch instructions can test the flags set by CMP following a comparison and transfer control to the appropriate address.

JUMP INSTRUCTIONS

The jump instructions alter the normal sequential processing of instructions and transfer control to the specified address, which is somewhere else in the program. This transfer is unidirectional, i.e., no return is expected; therefore, the return linkage is not saved. These instructions are analogous to Pascal's GoTo statement.

The 8088 processor allows two types of jumps—unconditional and conditional. The JMP instruction is used on unconditional jumps. On conditional jumps, branching to the specified label occurs only if certain conditions are met at the time the jump instruction is executed. If these conditions are not met, then no branching takes place, and the instruction following the jump instruction is executed.

Note that while all the conditional jump instructions test specific flags, none alter them; therefore, there are no flags affected following the execution of any jump instruction.

Unconditional Jump (JMP)
Flags Affected: none

As stated earlier, the JMP instruction causes unconditional branching to the label or address specified as the target. JMP does not save any return linkage; therefore, no return is expected following the branch.

Examples:

```
jmp 2DB7
jmp SHORT Exit
jmp NEAR PTR VideoInit
jmp Loop
```

If the execution control is transferred to an address within the current code segment, it is referred to as an **intrasegment jump**. This type of jump simply involves modification of the Instruction Pointer (IP) register to point to the new address offset.

Furthermore, even in this intrasegment jump, if the target is within 127 bytes of the current instruction, the jump is short-label, and the operand may be 8 bits long. If the target is greater than 127 bytes, the jump is near-label, and a 16-bit operand is required. For the most part, you don't need to worry about the short-label and near-label jumps since they are automatically coded by the assembler (or the compiler). You merely need to specify the label of the target instruction.

For example:

```
jmp TOP
```

This instruction will cause a jump to the label TOP, which may be anywhere in the program.

While the JMP instruction is most frequently used with labels, you can also specify the target address indirectly through a register or memory pointer. In both cases, 16-bit entities are required.

If the execution control is transferred to an address outside the current code segment, then it is referred to as an **intersegment jump**. This type of jump corresponds to a far-label jump and involves modification of both the CS and the Instruction Pointer (IP) registers to point to the new segment and offset.

Intersegment jump instructions use a 32-bit operand to specify the segment and offset of the target instruction.

Conditional Jump Instructions

As is evident in Table 6.2, there are 18 different conditional jump instructions, which test a variety of conditions to determine if branching should occur.

The general format of the conditional jump instructions is as follows:

```
Jcond <target>
```

In the above example, **cond** is the condition to be met for the jump to occur, and <target> is the new address where processing will begin if conditions are met. If the specified conditions are not met, sequential processing resumes with the instruction following Jcond.

Table 6.2 lists the various jump instructions and their descriptions. The flags that each instruction tests to determine branching are also listed.

For convenience and readability, several instructions have more than one form. Both forms can be interpreted as the same instruction.

Table 6.2

INSTRUCTION	DESCRIPTION	FLAGS TESTED
JAE/JNBE	Jump if above/jump if not below or equal	CF=0/CF=0,ZF=0
JAE/JNB	Jump if above or equal/jump if not below	CF=0
JB/JNAE	Jump if below/jump if not above or equal	CF=1
JBE/JNA	Jump if below or equal/jump if not above	CF=1 or ZF=1
JC	Jump if carry	CF=1
JCXZ	Jump if CX is zero	CX=0
JE/JZ	Jump if equal/jump if zero	ZF=1
JG/JNLE	Jump if greater/jump if not less or equal	ZF=0,SF=OF
JGE/JNL	Jump if greater or equal/jump if not less	SF=OF
JLE/JNG	Jump if less or equal/jump if not greater	ZF=1,SFOF
JNC	Jump if not carry	CF=0
JNE/JNZ	Jump if not equal/jump if not zero	ZF=0
JNO	Jump if not overflow	OF=0
JNP/JPO	Jump if not parity/jump if parity odd	PF=0
JNS	Jump if not sign	SF=0
JO	Jump if overflow	OF=1
JP/JPE	Jump if parity/jump if parity even	PF=1
JS	Jump if sign	SF=1

Following are some examples of conditional jump instructions. Each is preceded by the instruction that causes the respective flag(s) to be set, i.e., the flag that the jump instruction tests to determine whether branching will proceed.

```
cmp dx,di
jne START

cmp ax,FF
jne SETUP

mov cx,BUF_LEN
jcxz NEXT

xchg ax,cx
jcxz DONE
```

continued...

```
cmp WORD PTR COUNT,0
jbe EXIT

cmp al,F0
jbe INIT
```

SUBROUTINE-HANDLING INSTRUCTIONS

There are four instructions in this group provided to handle subroutine calls—CALL, RET, PUSH, and POP.

Emphasis here is not just on being able to pass control to a subroutine, as could be done using branch instructions, but also on being able to return control to the calling module (or instruction following the CALL). The program needs to know where to return. It also needs to preserve the environment for restoration upon return.

The following instructions in this group will be discussed:

CALL—transfers control to a subroutine.

RET—returns control following a call to a subroutine

The remaining two instructions—PUSH and POP—are used to save and restore the register (and memory) contents that may be altered by the called subroutines. They are also used to exchange paramaters with subroutines. These two instructions were discussed in the context of data transfer instructions in Chapter 5.

Calling a Subroutine (CALL)
Flags Affected: none

The **CALL** instruction allows you to invoke subroutines and return control to the calling module following the execution of the subroutine. CALL is analogous to the Turbo Pascal Procedure statements that perform the same functions.

Like the JMP instruction, a CALL may branch to a routine within the current segment (intrasegment call) or outside the current segment (intersegment call). The former is also considered a call to a NEAR proc, whereas the latter is considered as a call to a FAR proc, the primary difference being that a CALL to a NEAR proc results in a 16-bit return address saved on the stack, and a CALL to a FAR proc results in a 32-bit address saved on the stack.

The general format for CALL is as follows:

```
CALL <operand>
```

Here operand is a NEAR proc, a FAR proc, a 16/32-bit address in memory, or a register containing the address of the procedure to be called. Frequently, you will observe labels as operands for CALL instructions.

Returning from a Subroutine (RET)
Flags Affected: none

The **RET** instruction allows you to return control to the calling module following the execution of the subroutine. RET works with CALL to implement a subroutine call in assembly language.

Depending on the way the called procedure is defined (Near or Far), an intrasegment or intersegment return is automatically generated following the execution of RET.

LOOP INSTRUCTIONS

As the name suggests, Loop instructions are used to set up repetitive loops, analogous to Pascal's For..do and Repeat..until statements.

There are three instructions in this group:

- LOOP—transfers control to target if CX ne 0
- LOOPE/LOOPZ—transfers control to target if CX ne 0 and ZF set
- LOOPNE/LOOPNZ—transfers control to target if CX ne 0 and ZF not set

LOOP
Flags Affected: none

The **LOOP** instruction operates in conjunction with the CX (counter) register. You can even say that it loops as many times as the count specified in the CX register.

When Loop is executed, it decrements the value of CX by one, and transfers control to the target operand, which is usually a statement label somewhere in the program. The CX register is first decremented and then checked to see if it is greater than zero. Otherwise, control is transferred to the instruction following the LOOP instruction. In this respect, LOOP is analogous to Pascal's For..do statement, which also uses a count to set up a repetitive loop.

For example:

```
          mov  CX,StrLen      ;move length of string
          jcxz  DONE          ;get out if CX = 0
NEXTCHAR  ...                 ;read a character from string
          ...                 ;processing routine
          ...
          loop NEXTCHAR       ;loop to start of routine
DONE:     ...
```

LOOPZ/LOOPE
Flags Affected: none

LOOPE and **LOOPZ** are mnemonics referring to the same instruction. Like LOOP, this instruction also operates in conjunction with the CX (counter) register. The only difference is that it also checks the ZF flag as part of its condition for looping.

When LOOPE/LOOPZ is executed, it decrements the value of CX by one, and transfers control to the target operand, which is usually a statement label somewhere in the program. The CX register is first decremented and then checked to see if it is greater than zero. In addition, the ZF flag is also checked to see if it is *set*. If either or both conditions are not met, then control is transferred to the instruction following the LOOPE/LOOPZ instruction.

LOOPNZ/LOOPNE
Flags Affected: none

LOOPNE and **LOOPNZ** are mnemonics referring to the same instruction. Like LOOP, this instruction also operates in conjunction with the CX (counter) register. The only difference is that it also checks the ZF flag as part of its condition for looping.

When LOOPNE/LOOPNZ is executed, it decrements the value of CX by one, and transfers control to the target operand, which is usually a statement label somewhere in the program. The CX register is first decremented and then checked to see if it is greater than zero. In addition, the ZF flag is also checked to see if it is clear. If either or both conditions are not met, then control is transferred to the instruction following the LOOPNE/LOOPNZ instruction.

STRING INSTRUCTIONS

The 8088 instruction set includes a series of instructions dedicated to string manipulation. These "string" instructions enable you to directly move up 64K byte blocks of data from one memory location to another without first moving each byte or word into the accumulator. Other features of these string instructions include the ablility to scan a string for a specific value, initialize a string (block of memory) with a specific value, and compare two strings.

There are five principal instructions in this group:

- MOVS—move byte or word string
- CMPS—compare strings
- SCAS—scan string
- LODS—load string
- STOS—store string

Move String (MOVS)
Flags Affected: none

The **MOVS** instruction moves a byte (**MOVSB**) or word (**MOVSW**) of data from the memory location (string) addressed by DS:SI register pair to the string addressed by ES:DI pair. Both index register (SI and DI) are updated, i.e., incremented if the direction flag is zero or decremented if the direction flag is set. In other words, you can process a string forward or backwards, depending on the direction flag. See also CLD and STD instructions.

For example:

```
mov   AX,ScrSeg
mov   ES,AX              ;set up destination address
xor   DI,DI
mov   BX,B000H
mov   DS,BX              ;set up source address
xor   SI,SI
mov   CX,$07D0           ;set up counter
cld                      ;move forward
REP   MOVSW              ;move 2000 words
```

In this example, the source (DS:SI) is pointing at the monochrome display buffer. The destination is pointing at a storage area in memory. MOVSW moves a word (character and attribute byte) from source to destination. REP causes the MOVSW operation to be repeated 7D0 (decimal 2000) times.

Here also, MOVS is used in conjunction with REP to perform memory-memory block transfer. The CX register is set up as a counter containing the length of the block to be moved.

Compare String (CMPS)
Flags Affected: AF, CF, OF, PF, SF, ZF

The **CMPS** instruction compares two-byte (**CMPSB**) or word-size (**CMPSW**) values and updates the flags.

Specifically, CMPS subtracts the destination operand (addressed using ES:DI pair) from the source operand (addressed using DS:SI pair). None of the operands actually are affected. The result of the comparison is reflected in the flags. Also, the index registers are automatically incremented or decremented, based on the value in ZF.

CMPS can also be used in conjunction with REPE/REPZ and REPNE/REPNZ as follows:

```
repz cmpsb
```

This instruction compares byte-size values between two strings while they are equal (ZF=1) *and* end of string is not reached (i.e., CX ne zero).

Similarly, the instruction

```
repnz cmpsb
```

compares byte-size values between two strings while they are unequal (ZF=0) *and* end of string is not reached (i.e., CX ne zero).

See also CLD and STD instructions.

Scan String (SCAS)
Flags Affected: AF, CF, OF, PF, SF, ZF

The **SCAS** instruction scans a string for a byte-size (**SCASB**) or word-size (**SCASW**) value specified in the accumulator (AL or AX).

Specifically, SCAS subtracts the destination operand (addressed using ES:DI pair) from the accumulator (AL or AX register). None of the operands are affected. The result of the comparison is reflected in the flags. Also, the index registers are automatically incremented or decremented, based on the value in ZF.

SCAS can also be used in conjunction with REPE/REPZ and REPNE/REPNZ as follows:

```
repz scasb
```

This instruction scans a string for a (byte) value in AL while they are equal (ZF=1) *and* end of string is not reached (i.e., CX ne zero).

Similarly, the instruction

```
repnz scasb
```

scans a string for a (byte) value in AL while they are unequal (ZF=0) *and* end of string is not reached (i.e., CX ne zero).

Example:

```
   mov   AX,WORD PTR CS:[$2C]   ;get segment
   mov   ES,AX                  ;set segment address in ES
   xor   DI,DI                  ;point at first byte
   mov   CX,$1000               ;no of bytes to process
   cld                          ;set forward direction
   mov   AL,$24                 ;look for '$' char
repne scasb                     ;scan while not found
```

See also CLD and STD instructions.

Load String (LODS)
Flags Affected: none

The **LODS** instruction loads a byte-size (**LODSB**) or word-size (**LODSW**) value from the source (a string) operand addressed by the DS:SI register pair to the accumulator (AL or AX). Also, the index registers are automatically incremented or decremented, based on the value in ZF.

Store String (STOS)
Flags Affected: none

The **STOS** instruction stores a byte (**STOSB**) or word (**STOSW**) size value from the source (a string) operand addressed by the ES:DI register pair to the accumulator (AL or AX). Also, the index registers are automatically incremented or decremented, based on the value in ZF.

With the REP prefix, STOS can be used to initialize a block of memory with a specific value.

The following example causes the word-size value in the accumulator ($0720) to be stored at the memory location addressed by ES:DI. In this case, the location happens to be the monochrome display buffer. The AL register contains the blank character (hex 20), and the AH register contains the normal display attribute (hex 7). As a result of repeating this operation 2000 times (CX = 7D0H), the entire screen is blanked out.

```
mov AX,B000
mov ES,AX
xor di,di
mov al,20H
mov ah,7H
mov cx,7D0H
rep stosw
```

See also CLD and STD instructions.

FLAG INSTRUCTIONS

This group of instructions is used to manipulate individual bits in the flag register. See Chapter 3 for a description of the Flag (or Status) register and its bit flags.

The instructions in this group can be further divided into two subgroups as follows:

Flag Control Instructions

CLS	clear carry flag
STC	set carry flag
CMS	complement carry flag
CLI	clear interrupt flag
STI	set interrupt flag
CLD	clear direction flag
STD	set direction flag

Flag Transfer Instructions

LAHF	load flags in AH register
SAHF	store flags from AH register
PUSHF	push flags on the stack
POPF	pop flags from the stack

Flag Control Instructions

Instructions in this group are used to directly manipulate specific bit flags in the flag register.

Clear Carry Flag (CLC)
Flags Affected: CF

The **CLC** instruction zeroes the carry flag (CF).

Set Carry Flag (STC)
Flags Affected: CF

The **STC** instruction sets the carry flag (CF) to a 1.

Complement Carry Flag (CMC)
Flags Affected: CF

The **CMC** instruction toggles the carry flag (CF) to a 1 or 0.

Clear Interrupt-Enable Flag (CLI)
Flags Affected: IF

The **CLI** instruction clears the interrupt-enable flag (IF). As a result of this instruction, maskable interrupts are disabled. See Chapters 1 and 10 for further discussion of interrupts.

Set Interrupt-Enable Flag (STI)
Flags Affected: IF

The **STI** instruction sets the interrupt-enable flag (IF) to a 1. As a result of this instruction, maskable interrupts are enabled. See Chapters 1 and 10 for further discussion of interrupts.

Clear Direction Flag (CLD)
Flags Affected: DF

The **CLD** instruction clears the direction flag (DF). As a result of this instruction, string instructions auto-increment the index registers. See Chapter 6 for a discussion of string instructions.

Set Direction Flag (STD)
Flags Affected: DF

The **STD** instruction sets the direction flag (DF) to a 1. As a result of this instruction, string instructions auto-decrement the index registers. See Chapter 6 for a discussion of string instructions.

Flag Transfer Instructions

Instructions in this group are used to transfer the contents of the Flag register from/to the stack (POPF/PUSHF) and the AH register (SAHF/LAHF).

Push Flags on the Stack (PUSHF)
Flags Affected: none

The **PUSHF** instruction stores the Flag register on the stack and decrements the Stack Pointer (SP) register by a word.

Pop Flags from the Stack (POPF)
Flags Affected: all

The **POPF** instruction restores the Flag register from the word on the stack and increments the Stack Pointer (SP) register by a word.

Load Flags into AH (LAHF)
Flags Affected: none

The **LAHF** instruction loads the AH register with SF, ZF, AF, PF, and CF bit flags. These flags are loaded into bits 7, 6, 4, 2, and 0 respectively of the AH register.

Store Flags from AH (SAHF)
Flags Affected: AF, PF, CF, SF, ZF

The **SAHF** instruction loads the Flag register (flags SF, ZF, AF, PF, and CF) with bits 7, 6, 4, 2, and 0 respectively from the AH register.

INTERRUPT INSTRUCTIONS

These instructions transfer control (INT) to a specific service routine associated with an interrupt and return (IRET) following the execution of the service routine.

Interrupt (INT)
Flags Affected: IF, TF

The **INT** instruction invokes the interrupt type specified in the operand and transfers control to the interrupt service routine specified for that interrupt type in the interrupt vector table.

See Chapters 1 and 10 for more on interrupts.

Interrupt Return (IRET)
Flags Affected: all

The **IRET** instruction returns control following the point of interruption. It restores the Code Segment (CS), Instruction Pointer (IP), and Flag registers. IRET is used to return from Interrupt Service Routines (ISR).

See Chapters 1 and 10 for more on interrupts.

CHAPTER 7

CONVERTING ASSEMBLY LANGUAGE INTO MACHINE CODE

To use assembly language routines as Inline statements in your Turbo Pascal programs, you must convert them into machine code. This process is analogous to the function that the assembler performs on assembly language source statements and the Turbo Pascal compiler performs on the Turbo Pascal source statements.

The catch here is that you must perform this conversion manually, i.e., after you have written an assembly language routine, you must convert each statement into its corresponding machine code. Consider over 90 different instructions and many possible formats for each instruction, and you begin to sense how tedious this process can become.

However, with an understanding of the basics of machine language and the right tools, you can perform the conversion between assembly language and machine code with considerable ease.

There are several ways to convert assembly language into machine code for the purpose of inserting assembly language into the Inline statements. Some of the more commonly used ways are as follows:

- Using Debug's Assemble command
- Hand assembling individual statements
- Using some Inline code generation utility.

USING DEBUG'S BUILT-IN ASSEMBLER

Perhaps the most popular way to generate Inline code is to use Debug's built-in assembler. In Chapter 2, you were introduced to Debug's commands with a brief description of the **Assemble** command. If you recall, this command allows you to input assembly language instructions directly into memory. Debug assembles each statement one at a time. It supports standard 8086/8088 assembly language syntax for entering instructions.

Now enter a few assembly language statements in Debug, using the Assemble command. Follow these steps:

Step 1: Execute Debug

Step 2: Type A at the prompt, followed by <Enter> as shown in Figure 7.1.

Step 3: Enter the assembly language statements shown in Figure 7.1, each followed by <Enter>. Debug will automatically prompt you with the address of the next instruction.

```
C:\wp1\debug  <enter>
-a  <enter>
5870:0100  mov ax,3  <enter>
5870:0103  add bx,15 <enter>
5870:0106  inc bx  <enter>
5870:0107  sub bx,ax <enter>
5870:0109  <enter>
-
```

Figure 7.1 Assembling in Debug

As shown in Figure 7.1, when you type in the "A" command at the prompt, Debug requests input of an assembly language statement. The prompt contains, in segment:offset format, the current address of the memory location where the first instruction will begin. In Figure 7.1, the first prompt is

```
5870:0100          { Debug awaits input }
```

The input statement will be assembled in memory beginning at this location.

Debug initially sets the Instruction Pointer (pointing to the address of the first instruction) at offset 100 in the current segment; however, you can enter statements at any address by simply typing the new address.

For example, to begin assembling at offset 107, type the following command:

```
-a 107  <enter>
5870:0107              { Debug awaits input }
```

This command is useful for altering specific program instructions while executing them in Debug under its step-by-step Trace facility. You will see examples of this process later in the book.

To continue with the example in Figure 7.1, type in each statement followed by <Enter>. A return without any statement marks the end of input for Debug.

You can now use the **Unassemble** command to look at how Debug interprets each statement and also how it translates them. Figure 7.2 shows Debug's unassembly of the statements you typed in and displays the address of each instruction, its machine code, and the statement you entered. The machine code is displayed in hexadecimal format with each digit representing half a byte (a **nibble**).

```
-u 100 107  <enter>
5870:0100 B80300        MOV     AX,0003
5870:0103 83C315        ADD     BX,+15
5870:0106 43            INC     BX
5870:0107 29C3          SUB     BX,AX
-
```

Figure 7.2 Unassembling in Debug

As shown in Figure 7.2, the first statement

```
mov ax,3
```

generates machine code B80300.

Similarly, the second statement, ADD BX,15, generates 83C315, and so on.

Now trace each instruction and look at how it influences the values in the general-purpose registers. Invoke the trace faclility via Debug's **Trace** command. Type "t" at Debug's prompt as shown in Figure 7.3.

```
-t <enter>

AX=0003  BX=0000  CX=0000  DX=0000  SP=00EE  BP=0000  SI=0000  DI=0000
DS=5870  ES=5870  SS=5870  CS=5870  IP=0103   NV UP EI PL NZ NA PO NC
5870:0103 83C315        ADD     BX,+15
-t <enter>

AX=0003  BX=0015  CX=0000  DX=0000  SP=00EE  BP=0000  SI=0000  DI=0000
DS=5870  ES=5870  SS=5870  CS=5870  IP=0106   NV UP EI PL NZ NA PO NC
5870:0106 43            INC     BX
-t <enter>

AX=0003  BX=0016  CX=0000  DX=0000  SP=00EE  BP=0000  SI=0000  DI=0000
DS=5870  ES=5870  SS=5870  CS=5870  IP=0107   NV UP EI PL NZ NA PO NC
5870:0107 29C3          SUB     BX,AX
-t
```

Figure 7.3 Debug's Trace Facility

The first trace display in Figure 7.3 appears after the MOV instruction has been executed. As a consequence of this instruction, the value 3 is placed in the AX register, as shown in the display.

Similarly, when the ADD instruction is executed, you can verify that the value 15h is added to the contents of the BX register. Since BX was initially set at zero, it now holds the value 15 following the ADD.

The third instruction (INC) causes the value in the BX register to be incremented by 1.

Finally, following the execution of the fourth instruction (not shown in the above display), the value in AX will be subtracted from BX, leaving 13h in BX.

The whole purpose of this exercise in Debug is not to teach you how to use this utility but to familiarize you with some of its functions that you will rely on heavily in the process of interfacing assembly language with Turbo Pascal.

Also, note that the machine code (or object code) is actually the language that the 8088 processor understands. When programs are executed, these instructions dictate how the 8088 should process the data.

In the next section, you will look at the basic theory behind machine language coding, which will prove valuable to programmers who want to use assembly language routines in any language that supports inline machine code.

HAND ASSEMBLING INDIVIDUAL STATEMENTS

To incorporate assembly language routines within Inline statements in Turbo Pascal programs, you need to convert them into machine code instructions.

Fortunately, assembly language (being a low-level language) has a one-to-one correspondence with machine-level instructions. Each assembly language statement represents a single machine instruction, which is in contrast to Turbo Pascal statements that, as you saw in Chapter 2, generally represent several machine instructions per statement.

Earlier in this chapter, you saw several examples of machine code instructions (see Figure 7.2). For example statement **mov ax,3** generated machine instruction **B80300**. So far, these instructions simply appear as a series of numbers represented in the hex format. You need to find out what these numbers mean and how they are derived.

Machine Language Instructions

Each machine instruction is a series of numbers that specify the operation to be performed, the types of operand(s) being used, specific registers involved, and the addresses of memory-based operands.

These instructions also vary in length. They can range in length from one to six bytes. If you look at Figure 7.2, the first two instructions are three bytes long, the third is one byte long, and the fourth is two bytes long, as shown here. Remember, two hex digits represent one byte.

```
B80300        MOV      AX,0003
83C315        ADD      BX,+15
43            INC      BX
29C3          SUB      BX,AX
```

As you will see later in this section, the numbers and length depend on the type of operands used in an instruction as well as the operand addressing modes. The simpler instructions, such as INC, that operate on a single register operand are smaller (one byte), whereas a MOV that involves a word-sized (16-bit) memory-based operand may be up to six bytes long:

```
43              inc     bx
C7062000DB01    mov     word ptr [0020],01db
```

If necessary, refer to Chapter 4 for a review of operand addressing modes and Chapters 5 and 6 for a review of various types of instructions for the 8088 processor.

Machine Instructions—General Formats

When dissected, a machine instruction reveals several components, depending on its size. For convenience, these instructions are grouped into single-byte and multiple-byte instructions.

Single Byte/No Operand

There are two types of single-byte instructions: ones that do not have any operands, such as CLI (Clear Interrupt Enable Flag), and ones that have a single operand, such as INC (Increment). The instruction format for the no-operand instructions is quite simple. In this case, the eight bits represent the instruction's op code.

For example:

INSTRUCTION	OP CODE	
CLC	F8	(Clear Carry Flag)
CLD	FC	(Clear Direction Flag)
CLI	FA	(Clear Interrupt Enable Flag)

Single-Byte/Register Operand

The byte-size instructions with a single operand such as INC have eight bits to specify the operation and operand. In this single-byte version, INC operates on a register operand.

Note that INC also has a multi-byte format when its operand is memory-based. Here, you are only concerned with the single-byte version of INC.

The general instruction format for a single-byte instruction with an operand is shown in Figure 7.4.

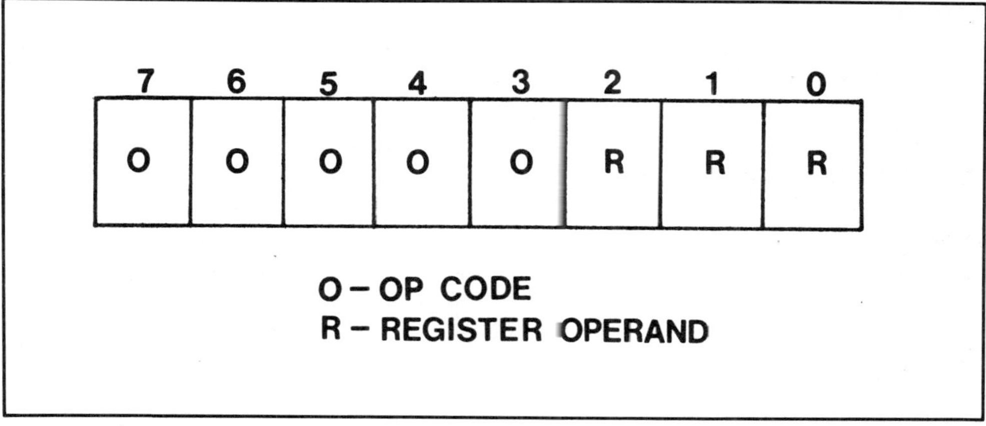

Figure 7.4 Single-Byte/Register Operand Instruction

Here, the five high bits (3-7) specify the op code and the three low bits (0-2) specify one of the eight registers—AX, BX, CX, DX, BP, SP, SI, and DI. Table 7.1 lists the bit values used to code each register and uses INC as an example to demonstrate how the machine code varies with the type of register used as the operand.

The op code for INC is hex 40 or binary 01000000. To get the actual machine instruction, add the op code to the register encoding value as shown in Table 7.1.

Table 7.1

REGISTER	BIT VALUES	MACHINE CODE
AX	000	01000000 40h
BX	011	01000011 43h
CX	001	01000001 41h
DX	010	01000010 42h
SP	100	01000100 44h
BP	101	01000101 45h
SI	110	01000110 46h
DI	111	01000111 47h

This format applies to all single-byte instructions. To derive machine code, simply look up the op code for that instruction in the Table (see Appendix C) and add the register encoding bits, if they apply.

You can test this process on your own by assembling these instructions in Debug and looking at the "unassembly."

Similarly, you can follow the instruction format to "hand-unassemble" the machine code and determine the instruction and its operands.

Two-Byte/Single Operand

For two-byte/single-operand instructions, the general format is shown in Figure 7.5.

Here, the op code is now shared between two bytes, with seven bits (1-7) in byte 1 and three bits (3-5) in byte 2 of the instruction code.

In addition to the op code, the low-order bit (bit 0) of the first byte also specifies the size of the operand. If it is a "1," then the operand is 16 bits wide; otherwise, it is 8 bits wide.

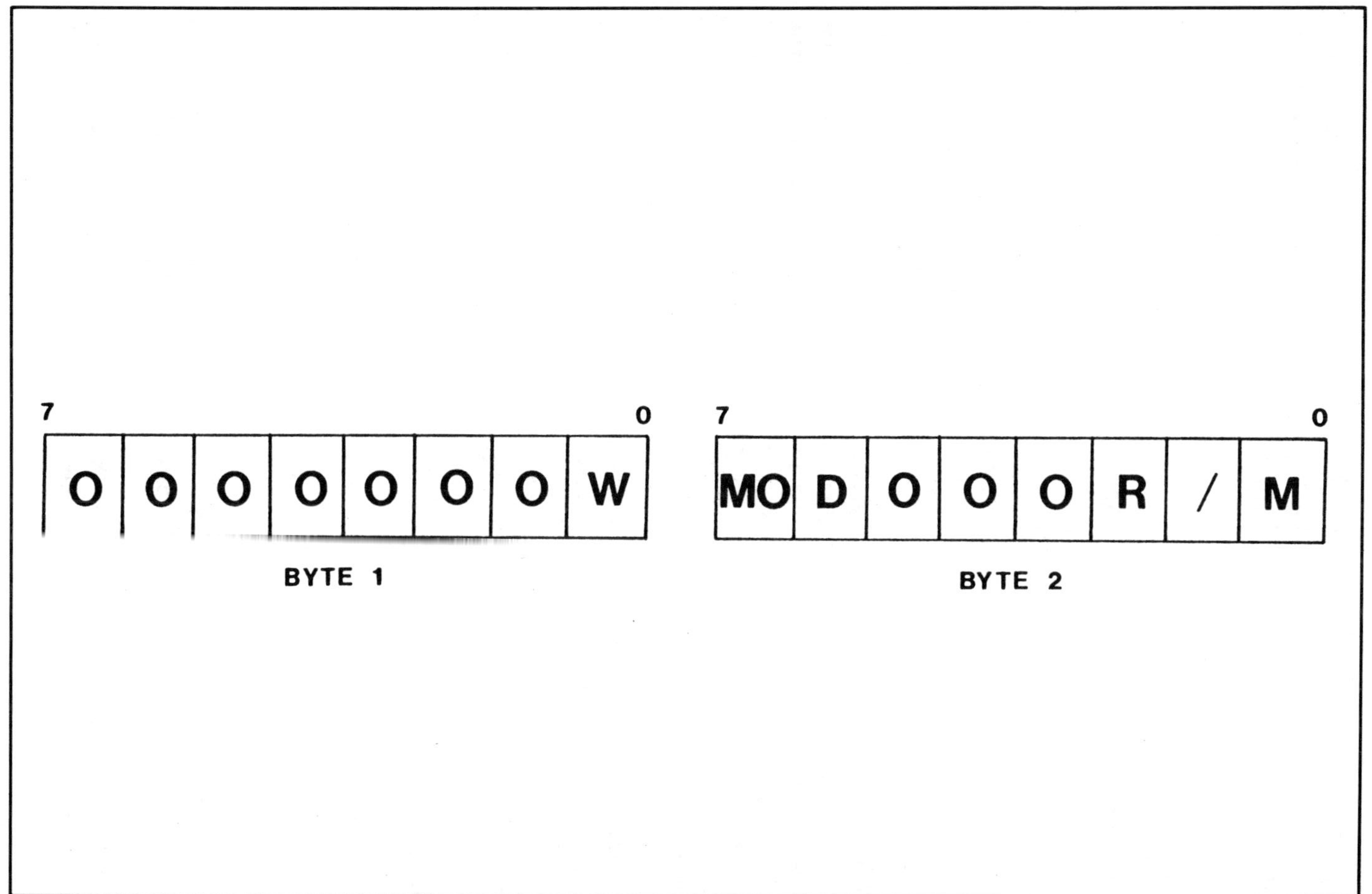

Figure 7.5 Two-Byte/Single-Operand Instruction

The high-order two bits (**MOD**) of the second byte specify whether the operand is a register or memory-based. The following bit patterns apply for the MOD field.

Table 7.2

MOD BIT PATTERNS	OPERAND
11	Register
00	Memory (no displacement)
01	Memory (8-bit displacement follows)
10	Memory (16-bit displacement follows)

The **R/M** field (an abbreviation of **r**egister/**m**emory), representing the low-order three bits (0-2) of the second byte, specifies the register type if the operand happens to be a register (MOD=11). The bit patterns for registers are shown in Table 7.3.

Table 7.3

REGISTER	BIT VALUES R/M
AX,AL	000
BX,BL	011
CX,CL	001
DX,DL	010
AH	100
CH	101
DH	110
BH	111

In the case of the first four registers, you will have to look at the zero bit "W" of the first byte to determine the size of the register involved.

Now, look at a few examples using the familiar INC instruction. This time, however, INC can operate on both register and memory operands.

The INC operating on an 8-bit register or memory operand has a different op code than the INC with a 16-bit register operand, which you looked at earlier. Here, its op code is hex FE or binary 11111110 in the first byte and 000 in the second. Sometimes, you will see this code represented as 11111110,000. Furthermore, if its operand is a 16-bit memory, then the first byte becomes 11111111.

The second byte will be coded depending on the operand used. If you use register BL, for example, the second byte becomes 11000011. The two high bits ("11") specify that the operand is a register; bits 3-5 are the second op code, and bits 0-2 ("011") specify the BL register; therefore, encode INC BL as follows:

```
INC BL          FEC3    11111110 11000011
```

You might try an exercise and code the following instructions on your own:

```
INC CX
INC DL
INC AL
INC DI
```

Remember that INC with a 16-bit register operand will still follow the earlier single-byte/single-operand format.

Now you know that to increment the contents of an eight-bit register costs an extra byte in instruction size.

For memory-based operands, the R/M field specifies the operand addressing mode. Remember that this field is used in conjunction with the MOD byte that specifies the **displacement** and the number of bytes to follow.

Displacement here refers to the one or two bytes following the two bytes of the instruction. These bytes specify the displacement added to the base register to determine the operand address. This displacement is an offset that is added to the contents of the base register specified as an operand. The general format of an instruction with one or two-byte displacement is as follows (see Figure 7.6):

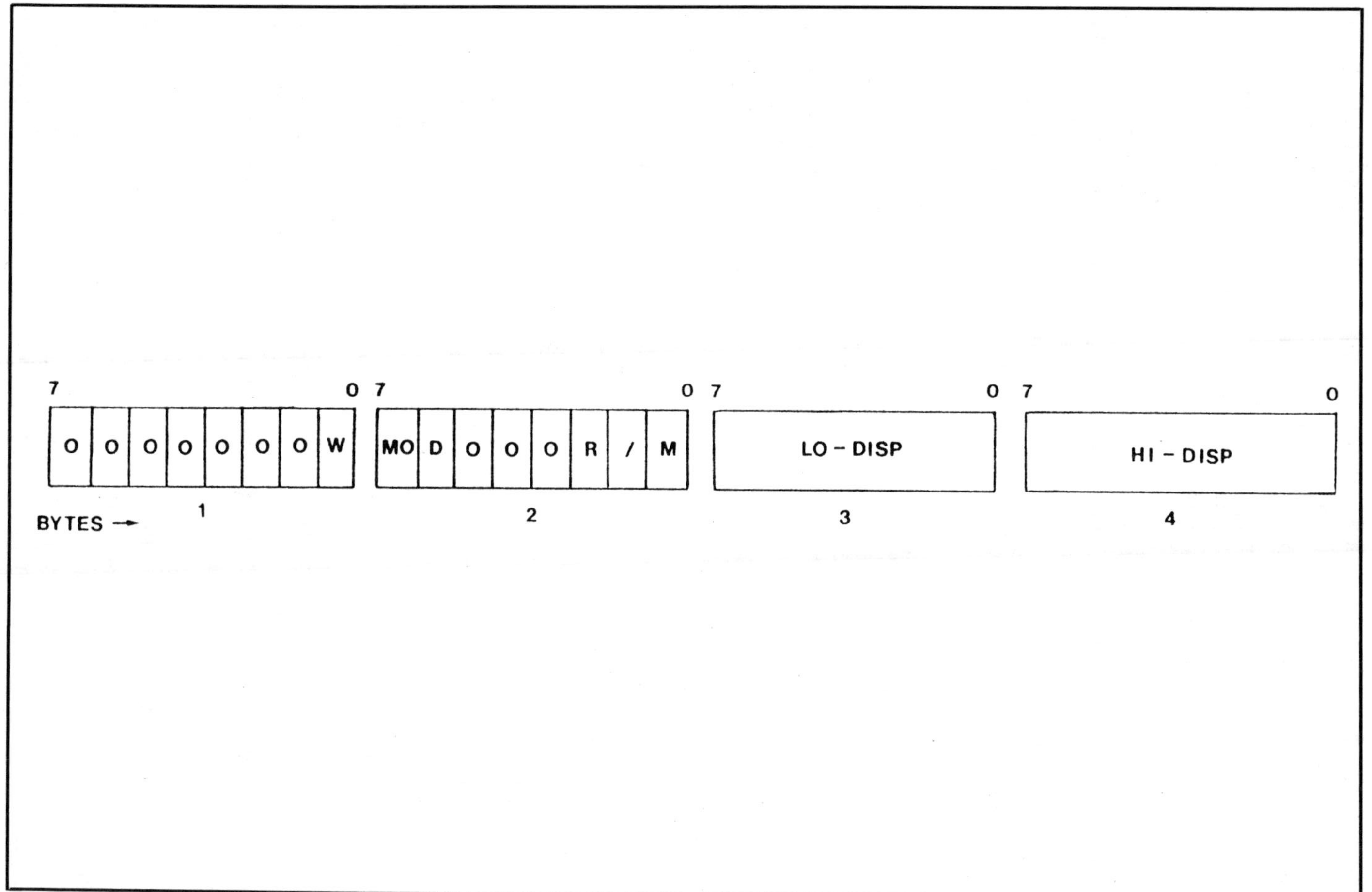

Figure 7.6 Displacement Encoding

You will look at a few examples of instructions using displacement values later in this section.

Table 7.4 lists the bit values corresponding to the various addressing modes.

Table 7.4

BIT VALUES R/M	OPERAND ADDRESS MOD = 00**
000	(BX) + (SI)
011	(BX) + (DI)
001	(BP) + (SI)
010	(BP) + (DI)
100	(SI)
101	(DI)
110	Direct Address##
111	(BX)

** For MOD = 01, add 8-bit displacement
For MOD = 10, add 16-bit displacement
For MOD = 01, [BP] + 8-bit displacement
For MOD = 10, [BP] + 16-bit displacement

Consider a few examples of INC used with a memory-based operand. As always, you will use Debug to assemble and unassemble the instructions.

Figure 7.7 demonstrates a sample session in Debug.

```
C:\wp1\debug
-a
5881:0100   inc word ptr [01ad]
5881:0104   inc word ptr [bx]
5881:0106   inc byte ptr [1ad + si]
5881:010A   inc word ptr [1ad] + [bp]
5881:010E
-u
5881:0100 FF06AD01       INC      WORD PTR [01AD]
5881:0104 FF07           INC      WORD PTR [BX]
5881:0106 FE84AD01       INC      BYTE PTR [SI+01AD]
5881:010A FF86AD01       INC      WORD PTR [BP+01AD]
```

Figure 7.7 Sample Session in Debug

In all of these examples, you are attempting to increment the contents of a memory location. As you can see, the type of machine instruction generated depends on how that memory location is addressed, as well as its size, which in Debug must be specified using the PTR operator.

In the first example, you address the memory location directly using its offset (or, in a program, the label). Debug codes this address offset as FF06AD01. The first byte FF (or binary 11111111) suggests an INC (FE) with a 16-bit operand (W = 1). The second byte 06 (or binary 00000011) represents the MOD (00), suggesting a memory operand, and R/M (011), suggesting a direct address. The following two bytes, therefore, are the low (AD) and high (01) bytes of the address offset.

In the second instruction, the value in BX is used as an address offset to the memory operand. Debug codes this address offset as FF07. Again, the first byte FF (or binary 11111111) suggests an INC (FE) with a 16-bit operand (W = 1). The second byte 07 (or binary 00000111) represents the MOD (00), suggesting a memory operand, and R/M (111), suggesting that register BX is the base register (containing the address of the operand) and there is no displacement, i.e., BX is directly pointing to the operand.

You can use the same technique to hand-unassemble the remaining machine instructions in Figure 7.7.

Two-Operand Instructions

Now consider the final group of instructions that require two operands. Obviously, one of the operands must be a register (for most of them); the second operand may be an immediate value, a memory-based operand, or another register. Examples of all three of these operands follow.

The general format for a two-operand instruction is slightly different from the two-byte/single-operand that you looked at earlier. Figure 7.8 displays this format.

The difference, as shown in Figure 7.8, is in the first byte where bit 1 (D) specifies whether the register operand is source (D=0) or destination (D=1).

Alternatively, when there are two registers as operands, then the bits 3-5 of the second byte are used to identify the first operand register.

In addition to these two formats, there are several other derivations based on this general idea. For example, an immediate-to-register move using MOV has the following format (see Figure 7.9):

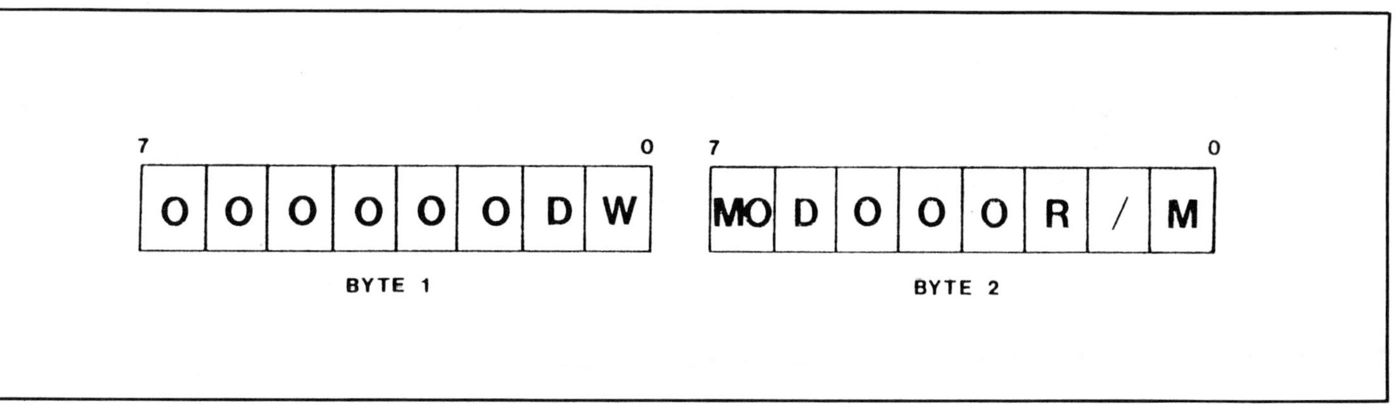

Figure 7.8 Two-Operand Instruction

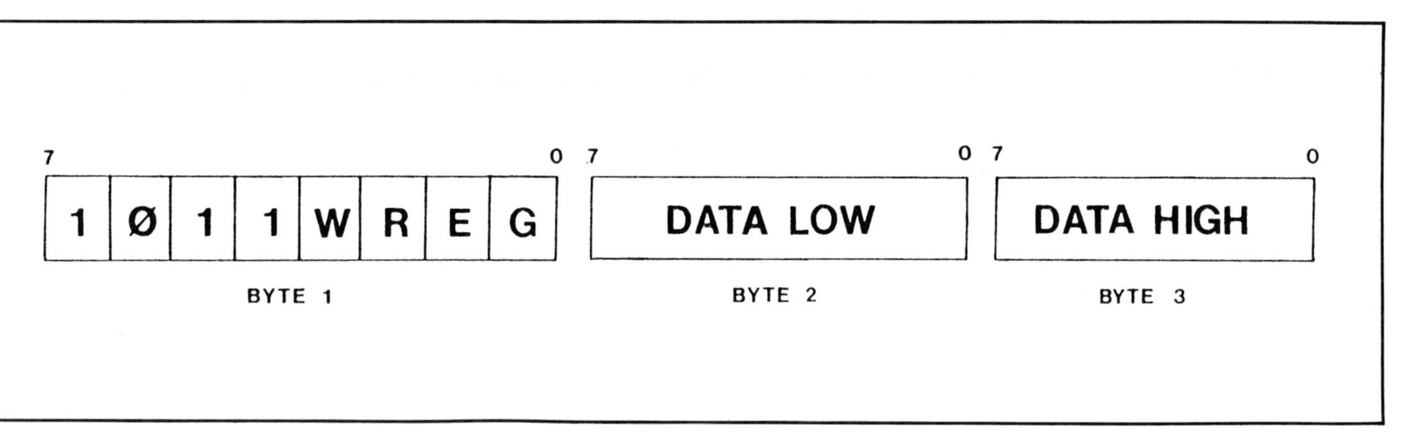

Figure 7.9 Immediate-Register Move

Not all of these specific formats have been covered in this chapter; however, once you begin to understand how the general instruction coding scheme works, you will be able to interpret an instruction set summary in any reference text and know how a particular instruction is to be coded. The idea here is to consider a few general examples to understand the basic theory.

In reference to Figure 7.8, perhaps the most common example of a two-operand instruction is the MOV instruction. Figure 7.10 presents a few examples of the Mov instruction with different operands and addressing modes. Once again, the display is generated from a Debug session.

```
-a
5890:0100   mov ax,1cb
5890:0103   mov ax,[0020]
5890:0106   mov ax,bx
5890:0108   mov ax,20 + [si]
5890:010B   mov dx, [bp] + [si]
5890:010D
-u 100 10b
5890:0100 B8CB01        MOV     AX,01CB
5890:0103 A12000        MOV     AX,[0020]
5890:0106 89D8          MOV     AX,BX
5890:0108 8B4420        MOV     AX,[SI+20]
5890:010B 8B12          MOV     DX,[BP+SI]
-
```

Figure 7.10 MOV Instruction Formats

The first instruction MOV AX,01CB involves the move of an **immediate operand** into the AX register. An immediate operand is one that is specified in the instruction itself. In this case, the first byte B8 (binary 10111000) specifies the instruction op code (1011), operand length (w = 1), and register (AX = 000). This instruction is a special case, and its format is shown in Figure 7.9.

The second instruction involves a memory-to-accumulator move. Similar to the first instruction, the second one also has its own format. In this case, the first byte, A1 (10100001), specifies the op code (1010000) and operand size in bit 0 (W=1). The remaining two bytes contain the address offset of the memory operand in the "addr low/addr high" order.

The third MOV instruction follows the general format discussed in Figure 7.8. Here, the first byte specifies the op code (100010,011), the size (W=1), and the register specified in bits 3-5 of byte 2 (the BX register) as a source (D = 0) operand. The second byte D8 (binary 11011000) specifies the second operand as a register (MOD = 11), identifies the first operand as register BX (REG = 011) and second (destination) operand as register AX (R/M = 000).

Segment Override Prefix

The offsets of operands in previous examples were assumed to be relative to the data segment, as is usually the case. If register BP is used as the base register, then the operand is in the stack segment.

There are cases, however, where you may want to override the assumption and specify the segment in which the operand resides.

Consider the following example:

```
mov [BX],AL
mov [BX],CH
mov [SI],AL
```

In this example, the operands are assumed to be in the data segment. If, however, they were located in the Extra Segment (ES), then you can specify the segment override prefix as follows:

```
mov ES:[BX],AL
mov ES:[BX],CH
mov ES:[SI],AH
```

In all of these cases, the base addressing is relative to the Extra Segment.

You will often see these instructions written as follows:

```
ES: mov [BX],AL
ES: mov [BX],CH
ES: mov [SI],AH
```

Both formats refer to the same instruction.

The segment override prefix causes an extra byte to be prefixed to the machine code. This "prefix" byte encodes the segment register, which is participating in the addressing mode. Figure 7.11 shows the structure of the segment override prefix byte.

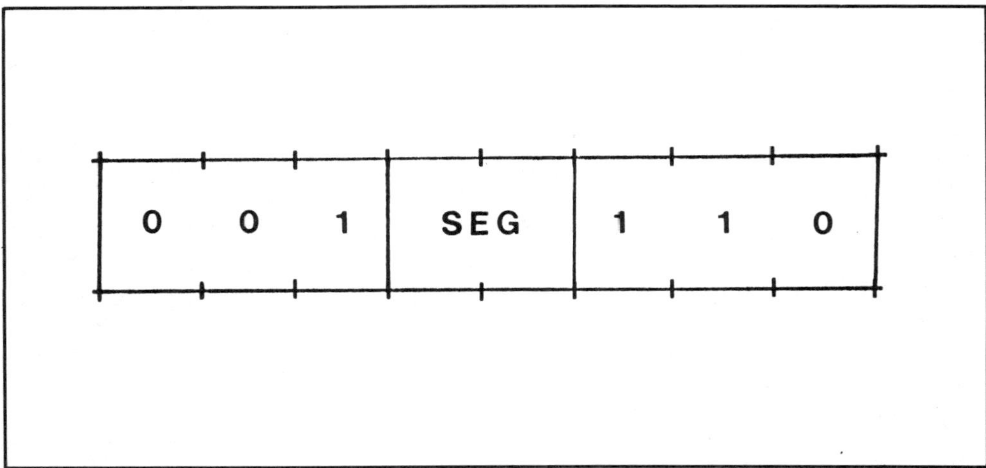

Figure 7.11 Override Segment Prefix

As shown in Figure 7.11, bits 0-2 and 5-7 show a pattern that characterizes this segment override prefix byte. Bits 3 and 4 denote the current segment in which the operand resides.

Segment encoding is shown in Table 7.5

Table 7.5

SEG	SEGMENT
00	Extra Segment
01	Code Segment
10	Stack Segment
11	Data Segment

Each instruction in the previous examples follows a predefined encoding format; however, as you have seen, there are quite a few of these formats. You do not have to remember all of these formats, as long as you know them and understand them. When you begin translating assembly language statements into machine code, you will mostly use Debug or some other translation utility. You will not be coding machine instructions one bit at a time. This discussion should help you understand the coding mechanism and explain the "method to the madness." Once you understand how the coding is done, you will be able to quickly code and debug the machine instructions in your Turbo Pascal programs.

INLINE CODE GENERATION UTILITY

Perhaps the easiest way to generate machine code for use in Inline statements is by using a program that does the conversion for you. INLINE.COM is such a program and is available in the Turbo Pascal data library (DL4) on Compuserve. Its author, Dave Baldwin, has also made the program source available to other Turbo Pascal users.

INLINE.COM reads an assembly language source file as input and produces an ASCII file containing the Inline statements that may be inserted into Turbo Pascal programs.

INLINE.COM has the following features:

1. Allows use of Turbo Pascal symbols within instruction entries (something you cannot do with Debug or an assembler).

2. Allows the use of labels for jump instructions.

3. Requires the '$' prefix for Hex entries, maintaining Turbo Pascal syntax.

4. Allows comments delimited by ';'.

5. Accepts a source file of up to 32K in size.

6. Allows up to 32-character-long symbols.

Figure 7.12 represents the assembly language source that is used as input by INLINE.COM. Figure 7.13 represents the output by INLINE.COM. You can insert this output directly into your program block that is to contain the inline statement.

```
              xor   BX,BX       ;clear register
              mov   AH,$01      ;kbd buffer check service
              int   $16         ;kbd input service routines
              jz    NOCHAR      ;Z flag = 1 means no character
              les   DI,[BP+>InKey] ;set up pointer to INKEY
              cmp   AL,0        ;Test for extended key
              je    EXTKEY      ;
           ES:mov   [DI],AL     ;get ASCII code
              jmp   SETFLAG     ;
EXTKEY:    ES:mov   [DI],AH     ;get scan code
SETFLAG:      inc   BL
NOCHAR: mov   [BP+>$08],BL ;set function result
```

Figure 7.12 Source Input for INLINE.COM

```
Inline(
  $31/$DB            {          xor   BX,BX       ;clear register}
  /$B4/$01           {          mov   AH,$01      ;kbd buffer check service}
  /$CD/$16           {          int   $16         ;kbd input service routines
  /$74/$13           {          jz    NOCHAR      ;Z flag = 1 means no char}
  /$C4/$BE/>INKEY    {          les   DI,[BP+>InKey] ;set up pointer to INKEY}
  /$3C/$00           {          cmp   AL,0        ;Test for extended key}
  /$74/$06           {          je    EXTKEY      ;}
  /$26/$88/$05       {       ES:mov   [DI],AL     ;get ASCII code}
  /$E9/$03/$00       {          jmp   SETFLAG     ;}
  /$26/$88/$25       {EXTKEY: ES:mov  [DI],AH     ;get scan code}
  /$FE/$C3           {SETFLAG:    inc   BL}
  /$88/$9E/>$08      {NOCHAR: mov   [BP+>$08],BL ;set function result}
);
```

Figure 7.13 Output from INLINE.COM

For more information on INLINE.COM and its associate files, you may contact Dave Baldwin at the following addresses (taken from the INLINE.DOC file):

SUMMER:	WINTER:
22 Fox Den Rd., Hollis, NH 03049	144 13th Street, East Tierra Verde, FL 33715

CHAPTER 8

INLINE STATEMENTS

Now that you have learned the basic theory behind assembly language and machine code, you can start applying it toward achieving the primary objective of this book—interfacing assembly language with Turbo Pascal.

As mentioned earlier, you can interface assembly language code with Turbo Pascal programs using one of three ways:

1. Insert machine code into the program within Turbo Pascal's **Inline** statement.

2. Call **External** assembly language routines. These subroutines are assembled outside of the program (thus called "external") into COM files using one of the available assemblers.

3. Call the assembly language routines that are part of the ROM-BIOS. These routines are provided so you can interface your programs with various operating system facilities and the PC's I/O devices.

Turbo Pascal provides built-in procedures—**Intr** and **MsDos**—that enable you to conveniently invoke the ROM-BIOS routines and DOS function calls respectively. You will look at these two procedures in Chapter 10 when invoking DOS and BIOS routines from within Turbo Pascal programs is discussed.

Which one of the three methods you choose to interface assembly language code with a Turbo Pascal program depends on what you want to accomplish in that program. You will examine the benefits and drawbacks of each method in this and subsequent chapters.

This chapter begins with the first and most preferred method—using Turbo Pascal's Inline statement. In Chapter 9, you will look at calling External subprograms from within a Turbo Pascal program and, in Chapter 10, you will see a few examples of situations where you are better off using one of the routines available as part of the ROM-BIOS services and DOS function calls.

In Chapter 7, various means of converting assembly language into machine code were discussed. Since this and subsequent chapters will rely quite heavily on machine code, you may want to review the appropriate topics in Chapter 7 before continuing with this chapter.

THE INLINE STATEMENT

Turbo Pascal's Inline statement allows you to insert machine code directly into your Turbo Pascal programs, into a procedure, into a function, or into the main program body. When compiled, this machine code becomes part of the program's executable code.

Also, because this is machine code, i.e., you have already hand-assembled it, the Turbo Pascal compiler does not perform any further conversions on it. As you will see later in this chapter, this code is represented precisely as it is in the compiled program (the *.COM file) and placed exactly where you insert it into the program.

Inline statements are written as follows:

```
Inline(code element1/code element2/...);
```

The Inline statement consists of the reserved word **Inline**, followed by a list of code elements separated by '/' and enclosed within parentheses, as shown above.

The code elements comprise the actual machine language instructions. Inline's components—the data elements—can be valid byte or integer constants or identifiers. The identifier may refer to a variable (global or local), typed constant, procedure, function, or parameter of a procedure or function.

Perhaps the real benefit of using the Inline statement in Turbo Pascal is that you can also use identifiers in Inline statements, which will be discussed later in this chapter.

The code elements can be expressed in both decimal and hexadecimal notations (following Turbo Pascal's rules on hex representation):

```
Inline($90/$90/$90);
```

The above example, also presented earlier in Chapter 2, shows the equivalent of the NOP instruction in machine code, represented in the hex format.

You can also represent it using an identifier as follows:

```
const
    NOP = $90;               { defining an identifier }

begin
    Inline(NOP/NOP/NOP);     { an Inline statement     }
```

Observe that this method is only convenient for simple, single-byte instructions. Such equivalents of op codes with Turbo Pascal constants can become complicated when you begin using instructions with a variety of operands, formats, and op codes.

Note that most programmers prefer to write the instructions in hex so that they maintain consistency with Debug and other similar utilities that also display unassembled program code in hex. Also, almost all references use hex notations to represent op codes for assembly language instructions. This format has been maintained when Inline code is presented throughout this book.

Like other Pascal statements, the Inline statement is quite free-form, i.e., there is no hard and fast rule about how it should be spaced or indented in a program; therefore, it does not matter whether the whole statement is written on a single line (if that is possible) or several lines. To the compiler, the whole program appears as a single long string of statements.

The most commonly observed format for writing Inline statements, as illustrated throughout this book, involves writing a single statement per line:

```
Inline(                { assembly language equivalent }
       $90             { nop           }
      /$B8/$12/$00     { mov   ax,12   }
      /$BB/$10/$00     { mov   bx,10   }
      /$41             { inc   cx      }
      /$03/$C1         { add   ax,cx   }
       );
```

In addition to the machine code, the equivalent assembly language statement is also included on each line, enclosed within curly brackets. The compiler treats these assembly language statements as comments, and they are used solely for reference. They aid in debugging, since you do not have to reconvert machine instructions into assembly language every time you attempt to debug the program. They also make it easy for readers to understand the Inline code since few have memorized the op codes.

Another frequently encountered and quite readable form of inline statements involves writing the equivalent assembly language statements separately, as shown here:

```
Inline($90/$B8/$12/$00/$BB/$10/$00/$41/$03/$C1);
{
  nop
  mov  ax,12
  mov  bx,10
  inc  cx
  add  ax,cx
}
```

The idea is still the same—to improve readability.

Here is an example of an unformatted Inline statement. Compare its readability with the one above, and you will see the difference.

```
Inline($90/$B8/$12/$00/$BB/$10/$00/$41/$03/$C1);
```

It is strongly recommended that you use the readable form of Inline statement with equivalent assembly language statements included as comments, as described above.

The Code Element

The Code element of an Inline statement consists of one or more data elements separated by '+' (addition) or '-' (subtraction) operators. The data elements may be one of the following types:

- Integer constant
- Local variable identifier
- Global variable identifier
- Typed constant identifier
- Procedure identifier
- Function identifier
- Function or procedure parameter identifier
- Location counter reference (*)

Depending on the type of data element and its value, one or two bytes of code are generated from each element following compilation. The following guideline applies:

If the data element is an identifier or a location counter reference (address at which the next instruction will be generated), its two-byte offset is coded into the instruction. If the data element is an integer constant, then its value will determine the size of the data element, i.e., a constant of value greater than $FF (decimal 256) will take up two bytes of code.

Note that if more than one data element is encountered, the actual value is determined by adding or subtracting the elements, depending on the signs that separate them. For example:

```
$A0/SCORES+4
```

If SCORES is defined as an array of bytes, then this instruction refers to the fifth element (address offset of SCORES + 4) of the array and moves the contents of the fifth element into the AX register, as shown in Figure 8.1.

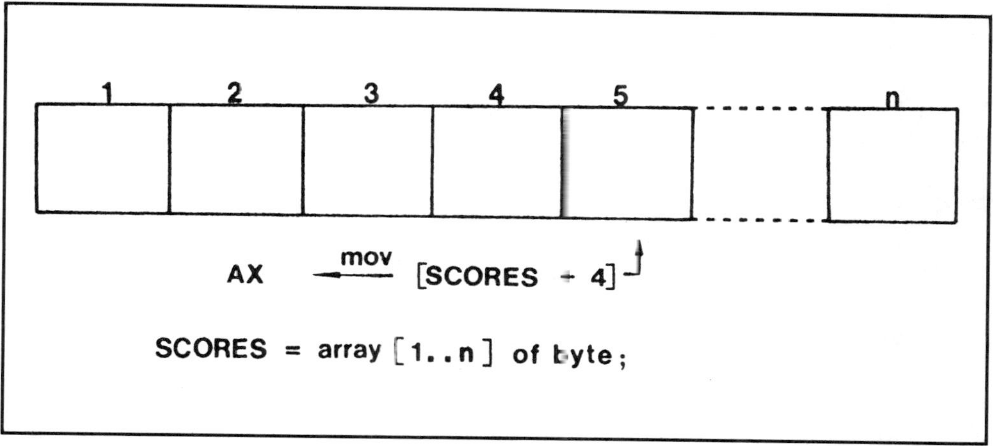

Figure 8.1 Addressing Using +/- Operator in Inline Statement

Note that here the compiler interprets SCORES + 4 as "4 bytes from the address (offset) of SCORES." The compiler does not add 4 to the contents of SCORES. If SCORES was defined as an integer variable that takes up two bytes in Turbo Pascal, the above instruction would be referencing some other variable in the data segment.

Similarly, if you define a String variable as STR, then the following instruction will move the first byte of this variable into the accumulator and subsequently into the CX register:

```
$A0/STR         { mov ax,STR     }
/$89/$C1        { mov cx,ax      }
```

This first byte is not STR[1] but is the length byte of the String variable (STR[0]). You may recall that this byte stores the current length of the string:

```
$A0/STR+1
```

The above instruction moves the first character of the string variable into the AX register.

These examples should give you some idea of how you can use the +/- operators to index and address elements in Turbo's data structures in Inline statements. Remember that when referencing identifiers, the actual addition and subtraction is applied to the offset address of these identifiers and not to the contents of the identifiers.

In contrast, when you reference constants in data elements, the compiler will add or subtract from the actual value of the constant. For example,

```
const
  X = $1A;

{ .. somewhere in an Inline statement }

$B0/X+4
```

This instruction will move $1E ($1A + 4) into the AL register. This move is treated as an immediate move.

Overriding Automatic Code Generation

The automatic code generation discussed earlier can be overridden by using the "<" and ">" symbols. The "<" symbol forces the code generation to a byte, and the ">" symbol forces it to a word. When the code element is forced to a byte size, the least significant byte (LSB) is used.

For example:

```
Inline(<$FA1B
     /$BB/
      $A52D
    />$43);
```

This statement will generate the following code:

```
$1B      { Forcing the element to byte size; using the LSB}
$BB
$A52D
$4300    { Forcing the element to a word; MSB filled with 0s}
```

Using Indentifiers in Inline Statements

The use of identifiers in Inline statements means that you do not need to be concerned with providing logical addresses of various data structures that you want to access in the Inline routines. During compilation, the Turbo Pascal compiler codes the appropriate address offset of the identifier, depending on its type.

Table 8.1 lists the various types of data elements and base registers used (as pointers) by the Turbo Pascal compiler.

As shown in Table 8.1, Integer constants are treated as immediate operands. The locally defined variables in a procedure or function are accessible from the stack through the BP register. The same is true for parameters that are being passed to the function or procedure that contains the Inline code. Variables declared in the main program (global variables) are in the data segment and are therefore accessible via the DS register. Typed constants are part of the code segment and are therefore pointed to by the CS register. The location counter refers to the address (offset) of the next instruction.

Finally, remember that you cannot access variable identifiers that are not in the main program body or in the current procedure or function. This rule not only applies specifically to Inline statements, but also to Pascal in general.

Table 8.1

DATA ELEMENT	BASE REGISTER
Integer Constant	None
Local Variable	BP
Global Variable	DS
Typed Constant	CS
Procedure	CS
Function	CS
Parameter of Procedure or Function	BP
Location Counter	CS

TURBO'S INTERNAL DATA FORMATS

When attempting to access data elements in an Inline statement, you need to know much more than the segment in which they are located; you need to know their internal data formats. This means knowing the size of the data structure as well as the way it is represented in memory.

Turbo's internal data formats are discussed briefly in this section. This information is also provided in the *Turbo Pascal User Reference Manual.*

Irrespective of where they are stored or whether they are part of complex data structures, Turbo's basic scalar data types have predefined sizes.

Char, byte, and Boolean values take up one byte in memory as do constants whose value is less than 256.

Remember that Boolean values can only be a 0 or 1.

Integers (and constants larger than 255) occupy two bytes in memory. Reals take up six bytes.

The size of a string variable is always one plus its length specified in the type definition. The first byte of a string variable (String[0]) contains the current length of the string, which also implies that a string length may not exceed 255. When the current length of the string is less than its specified length, you can assume that the remaining bytes are unused.

Pointers are addresses of variables located in the heap; therefore, they occupy a double word (4 bytes) in memory. The two least significant bytes contain the offset, and the two most significant bytes contain the segment address of the dynamic variable. A Nil pointer means low values (hex 0s) for both segment and offset address.

An array is stored as a linear structure, with the lowest indexed value stored at the lowest address in memory.

Similarly, records are stored in memory so that the first field occupies the lowest address in memory. The size of a variant record is the sum of the size of its fixed portion plus the size of the largest variant component. All variant components begin at the same address in memory.

Functions Seg, Ofs, and SizeOf

In moments of frustration, when you are experiencing trouble addressing certain data items, Turbo's predefined functions Seg and Ofs will come in handy, although their usage will definitely add extra code into your program.

Function **Seg** returns the segment address of its operand. The operand may be a variable, procedure, or function The result is an integer (two-byte) value indicating the segment address:

```
SegAddr := Seg(DisplayBuff);
```

Function **Ofs** returns the offset address of its operand. The operand may be a variable, procedure, or function The result is an integer (two-byte) value indicating the offset address:

```
OfsAddr := Ofs(DisplayBuff);
```

These functions are especially valuable in two instances:

- When you want to access specific data items in complex data structures. For example, you may want to manipulate a string within a record or a specific element of an array or table (multi-dimensional array). Both of these functions allow you to specify fields within records and subscripts within arrays. This specification eliminates any need for setting up complex addressing modes in your inline code.
- When you want to replace existing interrupt service routines with your own Pascal code. You can replace the interrupt vector with the segment and offset address of a subroutine, and control will be transferred to that subroutine when the interrupt is invoked. See Chapters 10 and 15 on interrupt service routines.

And, finally, when you are not sure about the size of an operand, you can use Turbo's function **SizeOf** to determine its size:

```
StrLen := SizeOf(Str);
```

This function is especially useful for untyped variables and complex data structures.

ACCESSING PARAMETERS IN SUBROUTINES

When you invoke a Turbo Pascal subroutine (function or procedure), all the parameters (or their addresses) to be passed to the subroutine are transferred to the stack. As indicated in Table 8.1, the Base Pointer (BP) register is used to access these parameters within the subroutine; therefore, when accessing these parameters within an Inline statement, you will set up addressability using the BP register.

For the most part, you can get away with including the variable name (identifier) in the machine instruction and let the compiler generate addressability; however, in some cases, you will want to know the actual locations of parameters on the stack.

This section discusses the various types of parameters and how they are stored on the stack.

First, there are two ways to pass a parameter to a subroutine–by reference and by value.

Passing Parameter by Reference

Passing parameter by reference simply means providing the subroutine with the address of the actual parameter, which most probably resides in the data segment. This address of the first byte of the parameter is pushed onto the stack in the form of a double word (4 bytes) during entry into the subroutine. You can move this address into the available address register pairs, such as DS:SI and ES:DI, either directly or via LES and LDS instructions. In addition to SI and DI, BX is also often used to store the offset address. For example:

```
Procedure ScanCode(var HexStr:Str6);

...somwhere in the procedure code

les  DI,[BP+HexStr]
```

This statement transfers the offset address of the string variable into the DI register and the segment address into the ES register. Following that transfer, you can access the contents of the variable using the proper segment override as follows:

```
ES: mov [DI],AX
```

Since passing a parameter by reference allows a subroutine to access it directly, you can assume that the subroutine can alter the contents of the actual parameter. If this passing occurs unintentionally, you should prepare for disaster.

Passing Parameter by Value

Another way of passing parameters to a subroutine is by value. In this case, the actual value of the parameter is copied onto the stack, and the instructions within the subroutine can move and process these values; however, they cannot access the parameter directly, so they cannot alter the value of the parameter external to the subroutine.

Note that larger data structures, such as arrays and records, are not transferred to the stack even when passed by value. In this case, you need to be aware of the fact that you only have their address on the stack.

The actual space that a parameter occupies on the stack depends on its size according to its internal data format, as discussed earlier in this chapter. For example, an integer will take up two bytes, and a real value will take up six bytes.

When byte, char, and Boolean-type values are stored on the stack, however, a word is transferred, even though the values only occupy one byte, because you cannot transfer a byte on the stack (see PUSH in Chapter 5). In the case of single-byte values, therefore, the least significant byte contains the actual value, and the most significant byte is left unused on the stack; however, you will still need to account for the presence of the unused byte if you are going to directly address the parameters on the stack.

Addressing Parameters on the Stack

In terms of addressing the parameters on the stack with respect to the BP register, the first parameter (also the rightmost in the parameter list) resides on the stack starting at address [BP+4], i.e., the fifth byte from the current location that BP is pointing to. From there, you can calculate the size of the parameter and the starting location of the next one by knowing the size of each. For example:

```
Procedure InKey(KeyCode:integer;Key:char);
```

In this example, Key will be at [BP+4], and there will be an unused byte at [BP+5] followed by a two-byte integer value starting at [BP+6].

Again, note that a string value will take as much space on the stack as specified in its type definition plus the length byte. Strings are generally accessed using a base register as a pointer.

Restore all addressing registers (CS, DS, and BP) to their original values when returning from a subroutine.

RETURNING FUNCTION VALUES

Since functions are subroutines that return a value, additional space is allocated on the stack to pass this value back to the calling block.

There are two points you need to know about returning values from functions:

1. The returning value is located at the top of the parameters, which is offset [BP+PARAMETERS]. You simply need to move the desired value into this location, and Turbo's run-time system will make sure that the calling routine gets the value.

```
Function Key(Inkey:char):Boolean;
```

In this example, the returning value is byte-size, located at [BP+6].

```
Function Translate(var StrIn):integer;
```

In this example, the returning value is word-size, located at [BP+8].

2. The size of the value depends on its definition. If a function is to return an integer value, then two bytes are allocated on top of the parameter list, and so on.

EXAMPLE PROGRAMS

Following are examples of two Turbo Pascal programs written using Inline machine code.

Program 8.1

```
Program UpperCase;
type
   Str20 = string[20];
var
   InpStr,
   OutStr  : Str20;

Procedure UpCase(var StrIn,StrOut:Str20);
{ converts a string into uppercase}

begin
Inline(
  $1E                { push DS                   ;save DS}
  /$C4/$76/<STRIN    { les  SI,<StrIn[BP]        ;set pointer to input string}
  /$26/$AC           {ES: lodsb                 ;get length, bump pointer}
  /$89/$F7           { mov  DI,SI                ;set addressability to ES:DI}
  /$88/$C1           { mov  CL,AL                ;move length to counter}
  /$30/$ED           { xor  CH,CH                ;clear high byte of counter}
  /$C5/$76/<STROUT   { lds  SI,<StrOut[BP]       ;set pointer to output string}
  /$89/$0C           { mov  [SI],CX              ;set length of output string}
  /$46               { inc  SI                   ;bump pointer to StrOut[1]}
  /$26/$8A/$05 { readchar: ES: mov  AL,[DI]     ;read a character}
  /$3C/$61           { cmp  AL,'a'               ;check for upper case}
  /$72/$06           { jb   nextchar             ;get next character}
  /$3C/$7A           { cmp  AL,'z'               ;check non-alpha}
  /$77/$02           { ja   nextchar             ;get next character}
  /$24/$DF           { and  AL,$DF               ;convert to lowercase}
  /$88/$04     { nextchar: mov [SI],AL        ;move character to string}
  /$47               { inc  DI                   ;bump pointer}
  /$46               { inc  SI}
  /$E2/$ED           { loop readchar             ;repeat if more characters}
  /$1F               { pop  DS                   ;restore DS}
);

end;

begin
   Write('Enter string up to 20 chars: ');
   ReadLn(InpStr);
   UpCase(InpStr,OutStr);
   WriteLn('Before conversion: ',InpStr);
   WriteLn('After conversion:  ',OutStr);
end.
```

Program 8.2

```
Program LowerCase;
type
   Str20 = string[20];
var
   InpStr : Str20;

Procedure LowCase(var StrIn:Str20);
begin
Inline(
  $1E               {   push DS               ;save DS}
  /$C4/$76/<STRIN   {  les  SI,<StrIn[BP]    ;set pointer to input string}
  /$26/$AC          {ES: lodsb                ;get length, bump pointer}
  /$89/$F7          {  mov  DI,SI            ;set addressability to ES:DI}
  /$88/$C1          {  mov  CL,AL            ;move length to counter}
  /$30/$ED          {  xor  CH,CH            ;clear high-order byte of counter}
  /$26/$8A/$05      {readchar: ES: mov  AL,[DI]  ;read a character}
  /$3C/$41          {  cmp  AL,'A'           ;check for non alpha}
  /$72/$06          {  jb   nextchar         ;get next character}
  /$3C/$5A          {  cmp  AL,'Z'           ;check lowcase}
  /$77/$02          {  ja   nextchar         ;get next character}
  /$0C/$20          {  or   AL,32            ;convert to lowercase}
                    {                            ;by turning bit 5 on }
  /$26/$88/$05      {nextchar: ES: mov [DI],AL   ;move character to string}
  /$47              {  inc  DI               ;bump pointer}
  /$E2/$ED          {  loop readchar         ;repeat if more characters}
  /$1F              {  pop  DS               ;restore DS}
);

end;

begin
   Write('Enter string up to 20 chars: ');
   ReadLn(InpStr);
   WriteLn('Before conversion: ',InpStr);
   LowCase(InpStr);
   WriteLn('After conversion:  ',InpStr);
end.
```

In the next chapter, you will examine a different, less popular way of interfacing assembly language with Turbo Pascal—invoking externally compiled subroutines. These subroutines are also referred to as **external** procedures in Turbo Pascal.

CHAPTER 9

WRITING EXTERNAL SUBPROGRAMS

In Chapter 8, you were introduced to three methods of interfacing assembly language with Turbo Pascal. The discussion focused on the first and most popular method —via Turbo's Inline statement.

The second method of interfacing assembly language with Turbo Pascal is through **external** subprograms. This chapter provides a brief discussion of this seldom-used Turbo Pascal facility.

External subprograms are compiled (assembled) outside of the Turbo Pascal enviroment; therefore, they are referred to as "external" subprograms. When you compile your Turbo Pascal program, the external subprograms (in binary format) are incorporated into the main program code at the point of declaration. Following compilation, they become part of the Turbo Pascal program in which they are declared as "external" subprograms.

CREATING EXTERNAL SUBPROGRAMS

External subprograms are assembled outside of the program into binary (*.COM) files using one of the available assemblers. If you are unfamiliar with the process, this section provides a brief overview.

For simplicity, an external subprogram can be viewed as a stand-alone assembly language program. The first step in the process of creating external subprograms for Turbo Pascal is to create the source. Certain rules apply for how you should write these programs and exchange data with them. These rules are discussed later in this chapter.

Once the source is created, you need to compile it to create an object file. This file—the output of the assembler—consists of machine code in binary ("undisplayable") format. The most popular assembler (and there isn't much choice) is MASM (Microsoft Macro Assembler) from Microsoft. To use this feature, you must own an assembler.

Following the "compilation" process, the object file is linked using the Microsoft linker. The output of this process is an *.EXE file.

The last step in this process is to convert the EXE file into a COM file using the conversion utility EXE2BIN.

Declaring External Subprograms

Once you have compiled an external subprogram into a COM file, you can declare it as a subprogram (procedure or function) in your Turbo Pascal program source. The declaration syntax is as follows:

```
procedure <proc name>(param list); external 'filename';

function <func name>(param list):type; external 'filename';
```

Note that unlike Inline machine code, which can be inserted anywhere in a subprogram block, external subprograms have no program block, no data declaration, and no statements; they only have the above declaration. This declaration tells the Turbo Pascal compiler that you want machine code from an external source inserted into the location of that declaration in the program.

Rules for Creating External Subprograms

There are three primary characteristics of an external program:

1. It is eventually integrated into the main program.

2. It is invoked (and therefore treated) as a Pascal subroutine (a function or procedure). The call can be from anywhere in the program block in which the subroutine is declared.

3. It must be able to communicate with the calling block, i.e., share and exchange data in the form of parameters.

In addition to these characteristics, there are a few rules to follow when creating the assembly source of an external subprogram.

1. The assembly language code must be relocatable. When the code is incorporated in the main program block, there is no telling where it will actually reside. That location results from where the code is declared in the Pascal program and what else comes before it.

2. All Turbo Pascal programs are activated with a NEAR (intrasegment) call (this may change with the large memory model). They also return with a NEAR return, i.e., only the Instruction Pointer is updated, and it is assumed that the code segment is still the same.

   The external subprogram must do the same, since it is also treated as a Turbo Pascal subroutine.

3. The external subprogram must restore the original CS, DS, SS, SP, and BP registers prior to executing a return (RET).

The following example provides the basic skeleton you need to set up around your assembly code:

```
code     segment
         assume nothing ; TP takes care of segment selection
                        ; no ORGing here
extern   proc   near    ; this is a must
         push   BP      ; save
         mov    BP,SP   ; params are on the stack
         ...            ; code
         ...
         ...
         mov    SP,BP   ; restore stack pointer
         pop    BP      ; restore BP
         RET    <return parm bytes> ; discard parms from stack

extern   endp
code     ends
         end
```

ACCESSING PARAMETERS FROM THE STACK

When a subprogram is called, the parameter's values (passed by value) or their addresses (passed by reference) are pushed on the stack. The order in which they appear on the stack is the same order in which they appear in the declaration, i.e., the leftmost parameter is pushed on the stack first. For parameters passed by reference, the segment address is pushed first.

You can assume that the rightmost parameter will appear closest to the stack pointer upon entry to the external subprogram.

To access parameters from the stack, you must know their internal data formats, which means knowing the size of the data structure as well as the way it is represented in memory. Turbo's internal data formats are discussed in Chapter 8.

Also, the stack pointer must be copied into the BP register to access the parameters as offsets of the BP register as shown in the example.

RETURNING FUNCTION RESULTS

Since external subprograms must remove all parameters from the stack before returning, there must be a way of returning function results.

According to the *Turbo Pascal User Reference Manual*, function results must be returned as follows:

- Values of scalar types (except reals) must be returned in the AX register. If the return value is less than 256, then AH should be zeroed.

- Boolean functions must *also* set the ZF flag as follows:

  True : ZF = 0
  False: ZF = 1

- Reals must be returned on the stack with the exponent at the lowest address.

- Pointer values must be returned in the DX:AX register pair.
- For complex data structures, it is recommended that you specify them as var parameters (pass them by reference).

CREATING AND MAINTAINING LIBRARIES

One of the principal advantages of external subprograms is that they can be grouped in a library, compiled to a binary file, and distributed to other Turbo Pascal users. The source code does not have to be provided to users for them to be able to use the routines in their programs.

Most commercial "program tool kits" provide libraries of commercial routines instead of inline source code. The best example of these libraries is the GRAPH.BIN file that comes with the Turbo Pascal compiler. This file contains a large assortment of graphics routines, which were written and compiled as external subprograms.

To create a library of subroutines, you must follow a two-step procedure:

1. Create a "jump table" at the start of the assembly language source that transfers control to the respective proc, as shown here:

```
InitVideo   proc    near
            jmp     InitVideo
            jmp     SetAttr
            jmp     SetColor
            jmp     ClearScreen

SetAttr:
        code for ScrAttr
InitVideo:
        code for InitVideo
SetColor:
        code for SetColor
.. and so on.
```

   Note that the actual organization of the procs in the library is not in any order.

2. In the procedure or function declaration, you need to specify the offset of the jmp instruction (3 bytes each) which transfers control to the proc corresponding to the function or procedure, as shown here:

```
Procedure InitVideo(.....); external 'VIDEO.COM'
Procedure ScrAttr(......); external InitVideo[3]
Procedure ClearScreen(....); external InitVideo[9]
```

You only need to declare as many functions or procedures as you intend to use in the program. The others in the library are ignored by the compiler.

EXTERNAL SUBPROGRAMS VS. INLINE MACHINE CODE

There are several reasons why Inline machine code is preferable to external subprograms when interfacing assembly language with Turbo Pascal:

1. For external subprograms, you must use an assembler, such as MASM, or a debugger that is capable of writing assembled code to a binary file.

   For Inline machine code, you can either hand-assemble the code using Debug or use a conversion utility such as INLINE.COM by Dave Baldwin. INLINE.COM is availble from various public domain sources.

2. In external subprograms, you cannot (directly) access program variables. For that matter, you cannot make direct reference to anything in the data segment.

   Inline statements can make direct reference to all variables accessible to the block in which they reside.

3. There are severe limitations on allocating work space for local variables in external subprograms.

   Inline statements reside within the main program block or within a procedure or function, so there is no limitation on declaring local variables.

4. The Pascal and assembler source code must be in different files. In contrast, Inline statements can be included anywhere in the program source.

CHAPTER 10

BIOS AND DOS SERVICES

In Chapters 8 and 9, you looked at two ways to interface assembly language routines with Turbo Pascal programs. In Chapter 8, Turbo's Inline statement was discussed, which allows you to insert directly into your programs assembly language statements in the form of machine code. In Chapter 9, you learned how to invoke externally assembled subroutines by declaring them as **external** procedures and functions.

A third approach to integrating assembly language into Turbo Pascal is simply to invoke external assembly language routines that are part of the system's BIOS. This time, however, these routines are pre-written and functionally specific; therefore, techniques and approaches involved in developing them do not need discussion here. You simply need to know what they are and how and when to invoke them in your programs.

These routines are part of the Basic Input/Output System (**BIOS**) that is hard-coded into one of the Read Only Memory (**ROM**) modules of the PC. They perform a variety of services primarily directed at providing an interface between DOS or an application program and the I/O devices.

As an example, when a Turbo Pascal program displays text on the monitor, reads keyboard input, or sends output to disk, it is actually invoking one of the BIOS services to perform the operations. You are generally not aware of this process (unless you peek at the program code in Debug) since you simply code Turbo's predefined procedures and functions in the program (source) to perform the I/O; however, during compilation (translation of the program into machine code), the compiler automatically codes these calls to BIOS routines or services.

You can also call any one of the BIOS services in your programs, using Turbo's predefined procedure—**Intr**. Intr automatically initializes the register with specified values, invokes the desired software interrupt, and returns the results (if any) of this invocation.

In addition to BIOS, DOS also provides many services that are used by applications. As you may have guessed, these services are themselves dependent on BIOS. They provide a more general-level interface while preventing you from directly accessing specific elements of the PC's hardware.

As with BIOS services, you can also access any one of DOS's services in your program via Turbo's predefined procedure—**MsDos**.

Both Intr and MsDos procedures will be discussed later in this chapter.

BIOS SERVICES

BIOS services reside somewhere in high memory, starting at hex paragraph F000H. For reference, you may want to refer to the memory map in the *IBM PC Technical Reference Manual* for a clear picture of the location of BIOS services relative to the rest of the PC's one megabyte of memory. The most recommended reference text for this discussion is the *IBM PC Technical Reference Manual.* It not only lists the various memory maps but also the complete documented assembly language source of the BIOS.

You will first look at how these services are invoked in a program (any program) and then at how you can invoke them in Turbo Pascal programs.

Invoking BIOS Services

The technique for invoking BIOS routines is quite similar to the way you call procedures in Pascal. Rather than using procedure identifiers, however, you pass the absolute memory address of the desired service (indirectly) to the **INT** instruction. This instruction, you may recall from Chapter 6, activates the service that corresponds to the interrupt number specified as its operand. INT uses the interrupt number to derive the address of the service from the Interrupt Vector Table.

The Interrupt Vector Table

The interrupt number specified in the operand of the INT instruction corresponds to a pointer table residing in low memory, starting at absolute 0. This table, referred to as the **Interrupt Vector Table**, contains addresses of BIOS services. In fact, it contains the four-byte address location of each of the interrupt services that are part of the ROM-BIOS. This address is in the SEGMENT:OFFSET format, with the first two bytes containing the offset and the last two bytes containing the segment of memory where the interrupt service routine resides.

Table 10.1 lists the interrupt vectors and their associate locations, as shown in a typical PC. These addresses may not all correspond with those in your PC since interrupt routines are commonly overwritten by applications that prefer to perform their own I/O operations. In other words, if you have a driver or RAM-resident program in memory, then some of these addresses will be different.

Table 10.1 BIOS Interrupt Vectors

INTERRUPT TYPE	SERVICE	ADDRESS OF THE INTERRUPT HANDLER
0	DIVIDE BY ZERO	00EB:3072
1	SINGLE STEP	0070:0147 IRET
2	NMI	F000:E2C3
3	BREAK POINT	0070:0147 IRET
4	OVERFLOW	0070:0147 IRET
5	PRINT SCREEN	F000:FF54
6	-- RESERVED --	F000:FF47
7	-- RESERVED --	F000:FF47
8	TIMER	F000:FEA5
9	KEYBOARD	F000:E987
A	-- RESERVED --	F000:E6DD
B	-- RESERVED --	F000:E6DD
C	-- RESERVED --	F000:E6DD
D	-- RESERVED --	C800:084E
E	DISKETTE	F000:EF57
F	-- RESERVED --	0070:0147 IRET
10	VIDEO I/O	F000:F065
11	EQUIPMENT CHECK	F000:F84D
12	MEMORY CHECK CALL	F000:F841
13	DISKETTE I/O	C800:0329
14	RS-232 I/O	F000:E739
15	CASSETTE I/O	F000:F859
16	KEYBOARD I/O	F000:E82E
17	PRINTER I/O	F000:EFD2
18	ROM BASIC ENTRY CODE	F600:FF53
19	BOOT STRAP LOADER	C800:01B0
1A	TIME OF DAY	F000:FE6E
1B	KEYBOARD BREAK	0568:00F2
1C	TIMER TICK	F000:FF53
1D	VIDEO PARAMETERS	F000:F0A4
1E	FLOPPY DISK PARAMETER	0000:0522
1F	GRAPHICS CHARACTERS	F000:0000

As mentioned earlier, and as illustrated in Table 10.1, the actual service routines are mostly located in the ROM, above hex paragraph F000H; however, as far as the applications requesting these services are concerned, these routines can be anywhere in memory. Applications can access any one of the routines by simply coding its number in the INT instruction. This instruction automatically looks up the address of that routine in the Interrupt Vector Table (Interrupt number x 4) and activates it.

When you perform I/O operations in a Turbo Pascal program using any of the built-in procedures and functions, the compiler automatically encodes the INT instruction in the compiled program code. You are, therefore, unaware of the process unless you try looking at the compiled code using a debugger.

Similarly, you can specifically invoke various BIOS services directly in your Pascal program using Turbo's **Intr** procedure. There also, the compiler will encode the interrupt call at the appropriate location in the program for requesting a specific BIOS service.

First, look at Turbo's Intr procedure for invoking BIOS services. You can then dissect it in Debug and look closely at the INT instruction that is coded by the compiler for activating BIOS services.

Activating BIOS Services in Turbo Pascal

As mentioned earlier in this chapter, Turbo Pascal provides the **Intr** procedure for activating BIOS services. Intr makes it convenient for you to invoke any interrupt service routine by simply specifying its number as its parameter (analogous to the INT instruction).

The Intr procedure also automatically preserves the program environment for you, which principally involves saving flags and registers. All you need to do is provide the procedure with the interrupt service type you want to access and a variable in which it can return the result of the interrupt call.

The general form of the Intr procedure is as follows:

```
Intr(Type, Regs);
```

where Type is the interrupt type selected from the Interrupt Vector Table (see Table 10.1), and RegSet is a data structure of the following type:

```
type
  Regs = record
            AX,BX,CX,DX,BP,SI,DI,DS,ES,FLAGS: integer;
         end;
```

The fields in the record Regs represent the 8088 registers, which are used to pass parameters to specific interrupt services as well as return the result of the execution of a specific service.

Since some of the 16-bit 8088 registers (AX, BX, CX, and DX) are also addressed as 8-bit registers (AL/AH, BL/BH, CL/CH, and DL/DH), you can redefine the above record type as a variant record to include both byte (8-bit) and integer (16-bit) length registers. This type definition will be as follows:

```
Regs = record
         Case integer of
           1: (AX, BX, CX, DX, BP, SI, DI, DS, ES, Flags : integer);
           2: (AL,AH, BL,BH, CL,CH, DL,DH : byte);
       end;
```

Following this record definition, you can access both register types for assigning parameters and accessing results of interrupt service routines. You will also frequently see the use of Turbo's **Lo** and **Hi** functions that return the low or high-order byte of the specified integer into an integer variable.

Look now at an example of the Intr procedure in Turbo Pascal.

Program 10.1

```
{ ------------------------------------------------- }
{ Program 10-1                    3/10/87           }
{ Author: Sanjiva Nath            Version 1         }
{                                                   }
{ Description: Demonstrating Turbo's Intr procedure }
{                                                   }
{ ------------------------------------------------- }
Program DetermineDisplay;

{ Use service 15 of Interrupt Service 10H to determine display type }

type
    Registers = record
                    ax, bx, cx, dx, bp, si, di, ds, es, flags: Integer
                end;
var
    Regs       :  Registers;
    Mode       :  Byte;
    Width      :  Byte;
    Page       :  Byte;
    DisplayMode:  String[20];

begin
    { Insert NOPs here }

    Regs.AX := $0F00;              { Requesting service 15 }
    Intr($10, Regs);               { Interrupt 10H -- ROM BIOS Video Services }
    Mode  := Lo(Regs.AX);         { Display Mode returned in AL }
    Width := Hi(Regs.AX);         { Screen width returned in AH }
    Page  := Hi(Regs.BX);         { Screen page returned in  BH }

    { Insert NOPs here }




   Case Mode of
        0 :  DisplayMode := '40 x 25 BW';
        1 :  DisplayMode := '40 x 25 Color';
        2 :  DisplayMode := '80 x 25 BW';
        3 :  DisplayMode := '80 x 25 Color';
        4 :  DisplayMode := '320 x 200 Color';
        5 :  DisplayMode := '320 x 200 BW';
        6 :  DisplayMode := '640 x 200 BW';
        7 :  DisplayMode := '80 x 25 Monochrome';
   End;

   ClrScr;
   WriteLn('Display type is ',DisplayMode);
   WriteLn('Screen Width = ',Width, ' Columns');
   WriteLN('Screen Page = ',Page);
end.
```

Program 10.1 invokes one the most frequently accessed interrupt services—Int 10H. This service, as you will see later in this chapter, is itself a set of 15 routines for controlling the PC's video display.

In Program 10.1, a special type of record (type Registers) is used to access the 8088 registers. In this example, the 16-bit registers are accessed. Later, you will also see some examples that use the variant record definition described earlier for accessing 8-bit registers.

Prior to the invocation of the Intr procedure, the AH register contains $0F, indicating the desired service number. As you may have guessed, service FH (15) of Int 10H returns the video display status. Specifically, it returns the current active display type code in the AL register, the screen column width in the AH register, and current active display page in the BH register.

You may want to compile this program in memory and execute it to confirm the output.

Now that you have seen the Turbo Pascal source code for invoking an interrupt service, look at the object code the compiler generated by unassembling it in Debug. Remember, you will want to set markers using the NOP instruction at the beginning of the program as well as at the end of the Intr routine, as indicated in Program 10.1.

Figure 10.1 shows the Debug unassembly of the marked routine, less the NOPs. At this point, you only need to appreciate the task that Turbo Pascal manages for you in allowing you to invoke the interrupt service routines. Later, this code will be examined in more detail and replaced with more compact Inline code.

```
329C:2DA2  B8000F     mov    ax,0F00
329C:2DA5  A36002     mov    [260],ax
329C:2DA8  BF6002     mov    di,260
329C:2DAB  1E         push   ds
329C:2DAC  E8B8E1     call   0F67
329C:2DAF  CD10       int    10
329C:2DB1  E8DBE1     call   0F8F
329C:2DB4  A16002     mov    ax,[260]
329C:2DB7  32E4       xor    ah,ah
329C:2DB9  A27402     mov    [274],al
329C:2DBC  A16002     mov    ax,[260]
329C:2DBF  8AC4       mov    al,ah
329C:2DC1  32E4       xor    ah,ah
329C:2DC3  A27502     mov    [275],al
329C:2DC6  A16202     mov    ax,[262]
329C:2DC9  8AC4       mov    al,ah
329C:2DCB  32E4       xor    ah,ah
329C:2DCD  A27602     mov    [276],al
```

Figure 10.1 Unassembling Program 10.1 in Debug

There are a few points to note in Figure 10.1. First, the INT instruction has been underlined. Interrupt service 10H is to be activated, and the compiler has coded that instruction in the program.

Prior to and immediately following the INT instruction are two CALLs to routines in Turbo's run-time library. If you execute the program under Debug's Trace facility, you will see that these routines appear to be saving and restoring the current environment.

In most cases, this save/restore effort by the compiler is excessive. Once you have carefully studied the specific service you want to invoke, you can create your own save/restore routines using Inline code, bypassing the code generated by the compiler. If you create the routines correctly, you can replace Turbo's code with a more compact and efficient code. Careful study is emphasized because if the environment is not restored properly, the program will likely crash, sending you into an orbital spin (especially if this happens in the wee hours of the morning).

Figure 10.2 presents an example of how Turbo's Intr procedure may be replaced with your own Inline code. In this case, you are accessing a specific interrupt service; therefore, you must take responsibility for saving and restoring the environment yourself. Compare the code in Program 10.1 with the code generated in Figure 10.2.

```
InLine(
  $B4/$0F             {     mov AH,$0F}
  /$55                {     push BP}
  /$CD/$10            {     Int 16}
  /$5D                {     pop BP}
  /$88/$46/<MODE      {     mov <Mode[BP],AL}
  /$88/$66/<WIDTH     {     mov <Width[BP],AH}
  /$88/$7E/<PAGE      {     mov <Page[BP],BH}
);
```

Figure 10.2 Calling Intr 10H Using Inline Machine Code

Reviewing the BIOS Services

Table 10.1 lists the BIOS interrupt services available on the PC. While all of these services are classified as software interrupts, they are often grouped on the basis of how they are invoked.

For example, services 8 through F are invoked as a result of interrupt requests generated by various devices, such as the system timer, keyboard, and floppy disk controller. The initial signal—a hardware interrupt in this situation—results in a call to one of the BIOS services; therefore, the process is often acknowledged as a software interrupt.

Several interrupt vectors in the table point to a dummy routine at 0070:0147 containing only an IRET (Interrupt RETurn) instruction. This instruction causes the control to return to the routine that requested the interrupt, without any action. These vectors eventually will be updated by DOS as a service is activated.

Following is a brief review of the range of BIOS services that you can readily access in your Turbo Pascal programs to directly control some of the I/O operations. There are eleven of these services, beginning with number 10H (decimal 16)—the **Video I/O** service.

Service 10H is a collection of routines that perform as many as sixteen different subtasks related to video display. These subtasks (or subservices) will be covered in considerable detail in Chapters 12 and 13.

Similarly, service 16H reads keyboard input, which will be covered in detail in Chapter 14 where various techniques for reading keyboard input in Turbo Pascal are discussed.

Descriptions of the other BIOS services follow.

Service 10H—Video I/O

Service 10H performs video I/O and provides status information on the type of display monitor (color or monochrome) in use, current display page, current cursor position, light pen interface, etc.

This service and its subservices or routines are briefly covered here. For details, please refer to Chapters 12 and 13.

Service 10H provides routines for the following:

Video interface (0,1,2,3,4,5,6,7, and 15)—these routines provide general interface to the video display adapter. Their assignments are as follows:

- Set the desired display mode (0)
- Set cursor type (1)
- Set cursor position (2)
- Read cursor position (3)
- Read light pen position (4)
- Select active display page (5)

- Scroll display page up (6)
- Scroll display page down (7)
- Status information (15)

Specific examples of these and the following routines are provided in Chapters 12 (text mode) and 13 (graphics mode).

Character handling (8, 9, and 10)—Routines in this group are provided to read (8) and write (9) character and attribute at the current cursor position and write character *only* at the current cursor position (10).

Graphics interface (11, 12, and 13)—These routines are used in the graphics display modes to set the color palette (11) and read (12) and write (13) dots on the screen.

Teletype output (14)—This particular routine provides a basic driver for writing a character to the display screen.

Each of the above interrupt 10H routines may be invoked by placing the appropriate number in the AH register. In cases where more parameters are required, other registers are also used.

Service 11H—Equipment Check

This service returns, in the AX register, the various peripheral devices that are attached to the system unit. In some cases (disk drive, game port adapter, and 8087 math co-processor), a specific bit (in the two-byte register) for a device is turned "ON" if that device is detected during equipment check. In other instances, the group of bits representing a device provides information on the specific numbers of those devices installed (printer adapters, RS-232 serial adapters, disk drives).

The bit representations for various peripherals are illustrated in Figure 10.3.

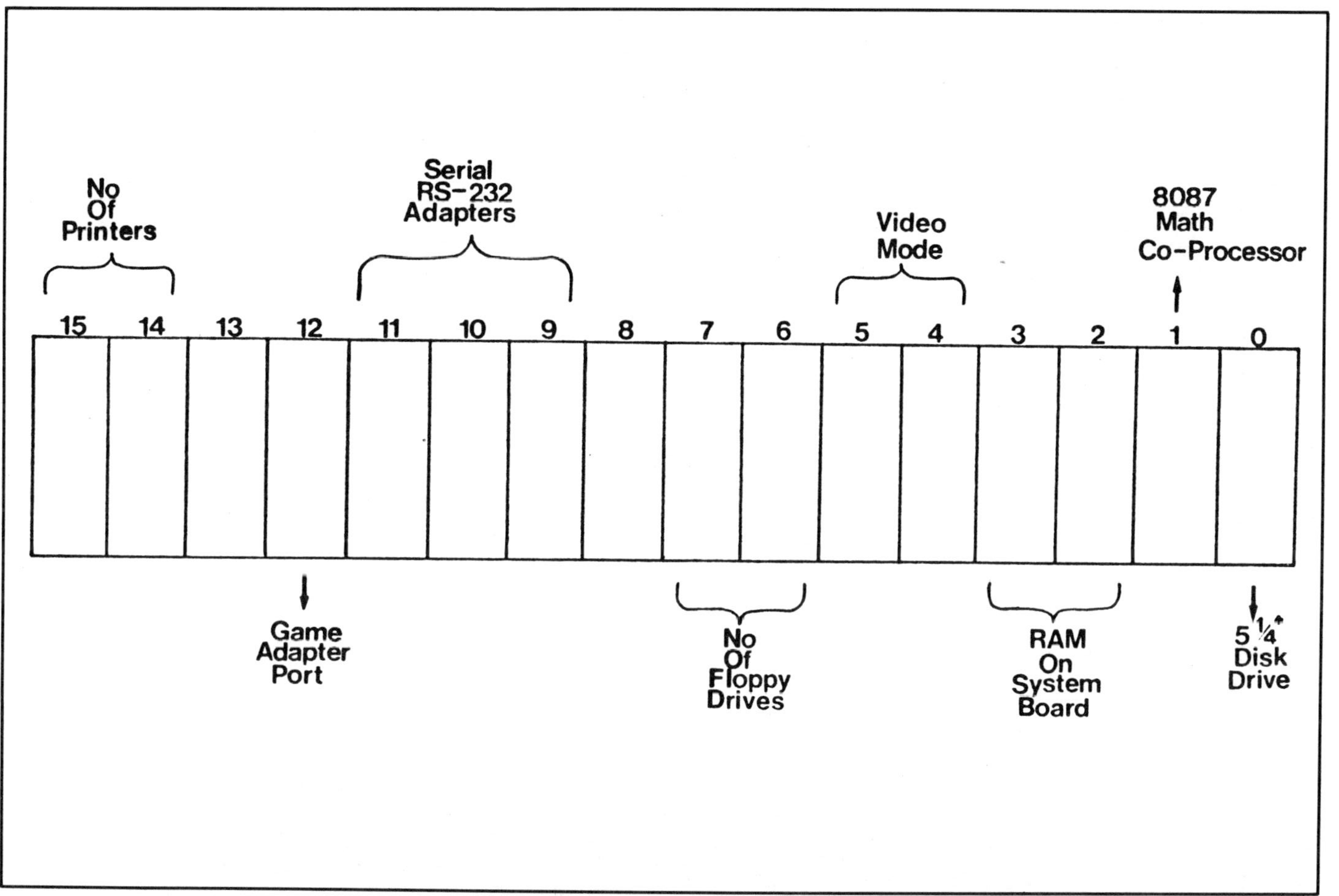

Figure 10.3 Bit Representation for Equipment Determination Bytes

This service is reliable only if you want to test for basic options, such as a parallel printer, serial interface, and disk drives. Beyond that, you can test this service with various configurations to see how it responds.

In addition to Service 11H, BIOS also provides routines that may be used to test for specific devices. For example, Service 15 of the interrupt service 10H can be used to determine the type of display adapter (monochrome or color) attached to the PC (see Program 10.1).

Finally, much of this information is also available in the BIOS data area, beginning in low memory at hex paragraph 40H. This section of ROM will be covered later in this chapter.

Service 12H—Memory Check Call

This service reports system memory in the AX register in the form of contiguous kilobytes (k) of memory.

Service 13H—Diskette I/O

This service provides several routines for accessing the 5 1/4" diskette drives. Similar to the Video I/O services, the individual routines are accessed by placing the appropriate value in the AH register.

Specifically, there are six routines available:

- Reset diskette system (0)
- Read diskette status (1)
- Read individual sectors into memory (2)
- Write sectors from memory (3)
- Verify specified sectors (4)
- Format the desired track (5).

Furthermore, services 2 through 5 also require parameters, such as drive number (DL), head number (DH), diskette track number (CH), sector number (CL), number of sectors (AL), and address of buffer (ES:BX). These parameters are appropriately passed to the individual routines through the registers indicated in parentheses.

Service 13H provides very low-level access to the diskette drives and the controller. This service is rarely accessed directly by application programs. Rather, DOS uses these routines to construct complex services that are more convenient for use by application programs; therefore, you will rarely see much emphasis on these services.

Service 14H—RS-232 I/O

This service provides useful routines for establishing communications with devices using the serial RS-232 interface. Most commonly, these devices include the modem and the serial printer.

As with video and diskette I/O services discussed earlier, individual routines are selected by placing the appropriate value in the AH register.

These routines support the following functions:

Initializing the communication port (AH=0)—the parameters required for initialization, such as baud rate, parity, stop bits, and word length, are specified in the AL register. AH returns the communication port status.

Send/Receive character over communications line (AH=1 and 2 respectively)—the AL register contains the character sent or received from the communications port, and AH returns the status of the operation.

Return communication port status (AH=3)—the AH/AL register pair returns communication port status. AH contains the line status, such as time out, parity error, and data ready. The AL register returns the modem status, such as DTS (data-set-ready), CTS (clear-to-send), and ring indicator.

Service 15H—Cassette I/O

No longer used.

Service 16H—Keyboard I/O

Three routines for reading keyboard input are available with this service. Like other services discussed earlier, these routines are accessed before calling the interrupt service by placing the appropriate number in the AH register.

The first (AH=0) reads the next character from the keyboard and returns the scan code for that character in the AH register and for the ASCII code in the AL register.

The second routine (AH=1) peeks into the keyboard buffer and sets the Z-flag accordingly, i.e., "1" if there is no character available and "0" if there is a character in the buffer. Furthermore, the character in the buffer is also returned in the AH register.

Finally, the third routine (AH = 2) in this service returns the current status of the Shift keys.

Refer to Chapter 14 for further explanation and examples of these routines, as implemented in Turbo Pascal programs.

Service 17H—Printer I/O

Service 17H provides routines for controlling output to a parallel printer. Since the PC is capable of supporting up to three parallel printers (ports LPT1:, LPT2:, and LPT3:), you can alternatively specify the printer that you want to access by placing the appropriate number (0,1,2) in the DX register. This number is a reference to the specific printer port address in the BIOS data area, starting at 408H. Three 2-byte words at this location are used to store the addresses of the printer ports, the first one being the default port, also used in the **PrtSc** (print screen) operation.

Routines available in this service allow you to print a character in the AL register (AH = 0), initialize the printer port (AH = 1), and obtain printer status (AH = 2), i.e., whether the printer is off-line, out of paper, etc.

This service is not commonly accessed in application programs, unless you are specifically developing printer driver routines. Perhaps the most common use for this service is to determine the printer status before directing any output to the printer because if the printer is busy or not responding, any print operation will cause the system to hang up.

Service 18H—ROM BASIC Entry Code

This interrupt service simply activates ROM BASIC.

Service 19H—Boot Strap Loader

Service 19H performs a **warm boot**, bypassing memory checking and device initialization routines; therefore, if any alterations are made in the ROM BIOS data area, they remain while DOS and application programs are "fooled" into accepting the altered system configuration because this service performs an **IPL** (initial program loading) operation, which loads DOS files as if the system is being powered up. DOS then initializes system memory and I/O drivers based on what it finds in the BIOS data segment, which is the altered setting.

Examples of subroutines using interrupt services to obtain information about the system configuration are presented at the end of this chapter.

Service 1AH—Time of Day

Service 1AH allows you to read (AH = 0) or set (AH = 1) the system clock. This clock is automatically updated by the 8253 System Timer at the rate of 18.2 counts per second via the Timer interrupt (INT 8).

As with several other services discussed so far, the clock count is maintained in four bytes, starting at hex 46C in the BIOS data segment. You can, therefore, directly read this value to determine the clock count between two processes, which gives you a means of determining execution times of various processes in a program.

For reading and setting the time of day, this service requires the high portion of the count in the CX register and the low portion of the count in the DX register. Since there are 1193180/65536 or 18.2065 counts per second, the count can be converted into minutes and seconds with precision. In fact, DOS also uses this clock count to calculate the time.

Special Vectors

In addition to the interrupt services described above, several vectors (1B through 1F) in the table have special significance (see Table 10.1). Some of these vectors point to data parameter tables for specific devices, whereas others are available as specific interrupts that may invoke user-defined routines. Following is a brief description of each.

Vector 1B—Keyboard Break Address

When you press the CTRL-Break key combination, interrupt 1B is activated, and control is transferred to the routine to which this vector points and, subsequently, is returned through the interrupt return (IRET) instruction. Under normal circumstances, DOS sets the address of the interrupt handler routine to terminate program executions and batch processing; however, this vector can be replaced by another pointing to a user-defined routine, and for each CTRL-Break key action, the new routine will be processed.

Vector 1C—Timer Tick

With each tick of the system clock, a call to interrupt 8 (Timer interrupt) is made. While Interrupt 8 responds to this call, interrupt 1C is also invoked. At power up, BIOS initializes this vector to point to an IRET instruction; however, this vector can be replaced with one pointing to a user-defined routine that will be processed with each tick of the system clock.

One simple example of this interrupt vector would be to use it for updating a software clock that constantly displays time on the display screen. Since you need to update this clock constantly, and also without manually interrupting other processes, you can use interrupt 1C to automatically interrupt the program with each clock tick and update the clock.

Vectors 1DH, 1Eh, 1FH—Pointing to Parameter Tables

The above vectors point to parameter tables for specific devices. Vector 1DH points to the area that contains parameters required to initialize the 6845 CRT Controller chip responsible for generating video display on both the monochrome and color monitors (see Chapter 12). BIOS automatically initializes these routines at power up to point to specific areas in the ROM; however, as expected, you can alter the individual vectors to point to any other area if you have dared to specify your own parameters for this and other vectors described below.

Incidentally, BIOS uses this table to set appropriate video modes, such as 40x25 color, 80x25 monochrome, etc.

Similarly, parameters required to control the operations of the diskette drives are stored in the location pointed to by vector 1EH, and, finally, vector 1FH points to the dot patterns of the second half of IBM's extended ASCII character set. These dot patterns are accessed in the medium and high resolution color graphics modes. Since this table is not in ROM, the vector points to a dummy area and may be replaced by the appropriate address when the user-defined table is loaded into memory.

BIOS Data Area

So far in this chapter, you have examined two of the BIOS segments—the vector table consisting of addresses of interrupt service routines and the BIOS code segment containing the code for the interrupt service routines.

A third segment is also of interest—the BIOS data segment. (This segment has been referred to on several occasions earlier in this chapter.) Beginning at hex paragraph 40H, this segment contains data that is frequently accessed and updated by BIOS and DOS. This segment is also available to applications through various interrupt services as well as through the quick and dirty method of direct access. Table 10.2 lists the addresses in the BIOS data segment and the data item available in each. Some of these key addresses are explored in detail in later chapters.

Table 10.2 BIOS Data Area (SEG 0040)

OFFSET	DESCRIPTION
0000	Addresses of RS-232 Adapters
0008	Addresses of Printer Adapters
0010	Equipment Flag
0012	Initialization Flag
0013	Memory Size
0015	Memory In I/O Channels
	Keyboard Data Areas
0017	Keyboard Flag 1
0018	Keyboard Flag 2
0019	Alternate Keypad Entry
001A	Pointer to Head of Kbd Buff
001C	Pointer to Tail of Kbd Buff
001E	Kbd Buffer
	Diskette Data Areas
003E	Drive Recalib Stat
003F	Motor Stat
0040	Timer Out Cnounter For Drive Turn Off
0041	Return Code Info For Stat
0042	Status Byte from NEC
	Video Display Area
0049	CRT Mode
004A	Columns
004C	Length Of Regen
004E	Buffer Addr
0050	Cursor Pos for Each Page
0060	Cursor Mode
0062	Active Page
0063	Base Addr Of Current Active Displ Adapter
0065	Setting of 3B8/3D8 register
0066	Current Palette
	Timer Data Area
006C	Low Word of Timer Count
006E	High Word of Timer Count
0070	Timer Rollover Flag
	System Data Area
0071	Break Key Pressed
0072	Kbd Reset
0074	Fixed Disk Data Area
0076	
0078	Printer Timeout
007C	RS-232 Timeout
	Extra Kbd Area
0080	Buffer Head Pointer
0082	Buffer Tail Pointer

DOS SERVICES

Like BIOS interrupt services discussed earlier, DOS also has its share of interrupt services that are mostly used by DOS during program execution. Although only a few of these interrupt services are currently being used, DOS reserves interrupts 20H through 3FH. Table 10.3 lists currently active DOS interrupts.

Table 10.3 DOS Interrupt Table

INTERRUPT TYPE (hex)	SERVICE
20	PROGRAM TERMINATE
21	DOS FUNCTIONS
22	TERMINATE ADDRESS
23	CTRL-BREAK EXIT ADDRESS
24	CRITICAL ERROR HANDLER
25	ABSOLUTE DISK READ
26	ABSOLUTE DISK WRITE
27	TERMINATE AND STAY RESIDENT

In addition to these interrupts, DOS provides many functions (almost 100 in DOS 3.xx) that perform disk file management, character I/O to various devices (such as the keyboard, printer, and display monitor), memory allocation and management, execution of secondary programs, and much more. With each new release of DOS, the function list grows. As stated earlier in this chapter these functions use BIOS services as building blocks to construct complex routines that are used by applications especially for disk-intensive I/O. While the use of these functions does not guarantee faster I/O, it does guarantee compatibility with other computers capable of running under the same operating system as the IBM PC but with significantly different architecture than the IBM PC.

All of these functions are grouped as subservices of interrupt type 21H, which generates a request to a specific function, based on the contents of the AH register. INT 21H is briefly discussed in the following section.

DOS Interrupts

In Table 10.3, eight DOS interrupt types are of primary interest. These interrupts are called in a Turbo Pascal program through Turbo's **Intr** procedure in a manner similar to the BIOS interrupt services discussed earlier. The only difference is that control is passed to DOS rather than BIOS. Also, as said earlier, most of the DOS interrupt services are used by DOS itself, and you will find little emphasis on these in the context of high-level languages like Pascal; therefore, they will only be described briefly, along with the relevant applications for some of these services in your Turbo Pascal programs.

Interrupt 20H—Terminate Program

Interrupt 20H terminates program execution and has been used as the traditional way of exiting from a program and returning control to DOS, which in turn transfers control to the address specified in the Program Segment Prefix (**PSP**) of the program returning the control. In Turbo Pascal, this exit routine is automatically coded by the compiler to request program termination.

Interrupt 21H—DOS Function Request

Interrupt service 21H provides a gateway to the myriad of functions available with DOS. When this service is invoked, control is automatically transferred to the specific function number specified in the AH register; therefore, to invoke a specific function, you can simply use Turbo's Intr procedure and assign the function number to the AH register. Depending on the function requested, other parameters also may be required in other registers. Turbo Pascal offers the **MsDOS** procedure for invoking DOS functions. This procedure will be examined later in this section.

Interrupt 22H—Terminate Address

When the program terminates, control is transferred to the address in this vector. This address may be a location in another program if the terminating program was running as a "child" process under a "parent" program; otherwise, control returns to DOS. Earlier in the discussion of interrupt 20H, the terminate address in the Program Segment Prefix was referred to, which is a 256-byte area at the top of every Turbo Pascal program that is executed as a COM file. The program terminate address is copied into the PSP before program execution. You may have already guessed from this discussion that this interrupt vector is solely used for storing an address, and is not used for generating an interrupt request.

Interrupt 23H—CTRL-BREAK Exit Address

This address also points to a routine to be invoked if the CTRL-Break key combination is entered from the keyboard during a standard I/O operation. The interrupt, therefore, is never actually generated in a program, and the vector is used solely for storing the address of a DOS routine.

Generally, DOS responds to the CTRL-Break key combination only during some I/O operations; however, if you specify the BREAK=ON command in the CONFIG.SYS file, DOS checks for the CTRL-Break command during standard I/Os as well as during most other function requests. Specifying this command allows you to terminate programs during execution by simply pressing the CTRL-Break keys. As expected, the added CTRL-Break checking tends to slow down some of the I/O operations, especially keyboard input. See Chapter 15 for more information on writing your own routines to service CTRL-Break interrupts.

Interrupt 24H—Critical Error Handler

A DOS critical error occurs in situations where a program attempts to write to a diskette with a write-protect tab if the drive door is open when a program or DOS is accessing it or when a printer is out of paper during a print operation. When such an error occurs, DOS transfers control to the routine specified by this vector. The critical error handler routine receives the AH register with the high bit set to a "0" if the error occurred during disk access; otherwise, it is set to a "1."

Furthermore, the register pair BP:SI points to the Device Header Control Block, which provides additional information about the type of device in which the error occurred. For more information on this control block, refer to the *DOS Technical Reference Manual.* This manual and other information on error codes returned by DOS for specific errors will be invaluable if you decide to construct a critical error handler in your Turbo Pascal program. See Chapter 15 for more information on writing your own routines to service DOS critical errors.

Interrupt 25H and 26H—Absolute Disk Read and Write

Interrupt services 25H and 26H provide low-level access to the disk with no consideration for the directory or individual files. In other words, you use these two services to read from and write to individual sectors on a disk without having to specify file names. These services are treated in more detail when various topics on DOS file management are covered in the next chapter.

Interrupt 27H—Terminate and Stay Resident

With the growing popularity of memory-resident programs, this interrupt service has generated quite a lot of attention from programmers and hobbyists. It is used to terminate a program that is to remain resident in memory, which generally means that when a program signals its termination through interrupt 27H, it also specifies a portion that is to remain resident. DOS marks the area of memory occupied by this portion of the program code so that other programs do not write over it. This portion behaves like a part of the operating system, and it remains in memory until the system is rebooted.

Termination of a resident program, therefore, is simply an indication to DOS that other programs may be executed although the resident program remains. The resident program can be activated using a common technique that assigns a key combination to that program and intercepts the keyboard interrupt service (16H) to first look for that key combination before passing the control over to another program.

Perhaps the preferred way of loading resident programs in memory is Function 31H, available through DOS interrupt 21H. This function allows you to load resident programs larger than 64k (which is the maximum limit with INT 27H) and also to pass exit codes to the parent program (or DOS). You can test these exit codes in batch files as well as in programs through function 4DH.

DOS Functions

DOS functions were mentioned earlier during the discussion on DOS interrupt 21H. To recap, these functions enable you to perform complex I/O operations without directly accessing the BIOS services, which maintains program compatibility over a wide range of computers that are capable of running under the same operating system, in this case, MS/PC DOS. These functions also enable you to exercise system-level control over program input/output functions.

Since these functions are numerous, only a general discussion of them will follow, with specific examples of a few.

For details on specific functions, refer to the *DOS Technical Reference Manual.*

Requesting a DOS Function—MsDOS

For convenience, Turbo also provides an **MsDOS** procedure that is specifically available for invoking DOS functions. The general form of the MsDOS procedure is as follows:

```
MsDOS(Regs);
```

where Regs is a record variable of the same type as described for the Intr procedure.

In addition, invoking a specific function requires the AH register to contain the function number. Many functions also require additional parameters, much like BIOS services discussed earlier. These parameters should also be placed in the appropriate registers before invoking a function.

A few examples are provided at the end of this chapter. Additional examples of functions are presented in various contexts throughout this book.

Check DOS Version

This function invokes DOS service 30H of Intr 21H to get the version of DOS in use. On return from Intr 21H, the register assignments are as follows:

AL = Major version
AH = Minor version

Function DOS3 checks for DOS 3.0 or higher. It returns a Boolean True if DOS version is 3.0 or higher. You can add parameters to this function to also get the major and minor versions. Don't forget to update the offset for the function result.

```
Function DOS3:Boolean;
begin
Inline(
  $30/$DB            {         xor  bl,bl}
  /$B4/$30           {         mov  AH,$30   ;function 30H Get DOS Vers}
  /$CD/$21           {         int  $21      ;DOS interrupt 21H}
  /$3C/$03           {         cmp  AL,3     ;check if vers 3}
  /$72/$02           {         jb   DONE     ;if not then get out}
  /$FE/$C3           {         inc  BL       ;else set up Boolean value}
  /$88/$9E/>4        {    DONE:mov  [BP+$4],BL ;set function result}
);
end;
```

Sample program using this function:

```
:
Program CheckDosVers;

{$I DOSVERS.INC}  { function above }

begin
   If DOS3  then
      Write('DOS Version 3.0 or higher')
   else
      Write('Pre DOS 3.0 version ');
end.
```

Check 8087 Math CoProcessor

This function invokes BIOS Intr 11H (equipment determination) to check the presence of the 8087 numeric coprocessor.

On return, the AX register contains the equipment flags. Bit 1 of AL is set if 8087 is detected.

Function MathChip checks for 8087. It returns a Boolean True if the 8087 is detected.

```
Function MathChip:Boolean;
begin
Inline(
  $30/$DB        {        xor  bl,bl    ;clearing function result}
  /$CD/$11          {         int  $11       ;BIOS interrupt 11H (Equip
Check)}
  /$A8/$02       {        test AL,2     ;check if 8087 installed}
  /$74/$02       {        jz   DONE     ;if not then get out}
  /$FE/$C3       {        inc  BL       ;else set up Boolean value}
  /$88/$9E/>4    {   DONE:mov  [BP+>4],BL ;set function result}
);
end;
```

This function is an example of how you can use the equipment determination flag to check for various devices.

Time of Day

This function invokes DOS service 2CH (Time Of Day) of Intr 21H to get the time in hours, minutes, seconds, and hundredths of seconds. On return from Intr 21H, the register assignments are as follows:

CH = Hours
CL = Minutes
DH = Seconds
DL = Hundredths

Function TimeODay gets the time in hours and minutes.

```
Function TimeODay:integer;
begin
Inline(
  $B4/$2C          {       mov  AH,$2C   ;function 30H Time Of Day}
  /$CD/$21         {       int  $21      ;DOS interrupt 21H}
  /$88/$6E/<5      {       mov  [BP+<5],CH ;hours}
  /$88/$4E/<4      {       mov  [BP+<4],CL ;minutes}
);
end;
```

The function returns an integer value that contains the hour in the most significant byte and minutes in the least significant byte. You can change this format to suit your applications.

In the next chapter, you will look at various techniques for reading keyboard input in Turbo Pascal, using both of Turbo's built-in subroutines as well as using Inline code.

CHAPTER 11

MEMORY AND DISK FILE MANAGEMENT

The Turbo Pascal compiler has many built-in facilities to automatically interface programs with the operating system, whether that system is PC-DOS, CP/M-86, CP/M-80, or any other system for which future versions of Turbo Pascal may offer support. These facilities allow you to load and execute Turbo-compiled programs in memory and perform many common I/O operations.

Each of these facilities is a complex series of instructions automatically encoded into your programs by the Turbo Pascal compiler. If Turbo did not offer support for them, you would have to manually code them into your programs. While Turbo is not unique in this aspect (most high-level languages offer some support), Turbo excels in these facilities.

Like other high-level languages, Turbo Pascal allows you to develop programs that automatically interface with the operating system to perform fancy I/O with devices. For the most part, you do not have to understand the actual input/output mechanisms.

While these built-in facilities exist in Turbo Pascal, it is important (although not necessary) to understand how a program interfaces with the operating system. A basic understanding of the operating system environment in which your programs execute gives you the edge you need to develop efficient and sophisticated applications. In this chapter, some of the important aspects of the DOS environment are briefly covered, with focus on PC-DOS, specifically versions 2.1 and 3.1.

Primarily, there are two facets of the operating system environment that need classification here:

- memory management
- disk file management

Memory management refers to the way DOS organizes the PC's memory, i.e., where it keeps control and supervisory modules, where it loads the application programs (COM files), and so on.

Similarly, **disk file management** refers to the way DOS organizes data on a disk (or diskette) for storage, retrieval, and updates. The two topics are unrelated, although they are discussed together in this chapter. They share the operating system environment and influence the same programs. Before beginning to discuss each topic, however, you should examine the components of DOS more closely.

DOS COMPONENTS

You are probably familiar with the essential components of PC DOS. Physically, there are three files—IBMBIO.COM, IBMDOS.COM, and COMMAND.COM—that are available on the DOS system diskette.

IBMBIO.COM is an extension of ROM-BIOS. It provides a convenient means of replacing, relocating, and adding BIOS services for I/O devices. It initializes attached devices and transfers control to DOS once the IBMDOS.COM is loaded into the appropriate areas of memory.

IBMDOS.COM contains the actual disk operating system program. It provides a high-level interface to various I/O devices as well as file and memory management services through a variety of interrupt services and function requests for your programs. DOS reserves interrupts 20H to 3FH for its own use, although only a few of these are currently used for invoking services. DOS uses interrupt 21H as an entry point for function requests.

COMMAND.COM contains the command processor—the supervisor program that examines the commands entered at the keyboard and invokes DOS internal and external commands as well as any external program commands. COMMAND.COM looks for an external program file in specified drives and directories and loads it at the appropriate location in memory, depending on the format of the file (BAT, EXE, or COM file). For all practical purposes, you need only consider the COM file because Turbo Pascal only creates a COM file as a compiled output.

COMMAND.COM also processes interrupt types 22H through 24H (the program terminate address, the Ctrl-Break processor, and the critical error handler respectively). It is also responsible for processing the AUTOEXEC.BAT file upon system startup and produces the familiar DOS prompt "A" (or whatever drive is currently active).

DOS Memory Management

Memory management is probably the topic of least concern to you because you are using a high-level language—Turbo Pascal. Both DOS and the Turbo Pascal compiler handle most of the memory management tasks such as loading and executing programs, allocating memory for program and data areas, stack and heap management, and so forth.

Memory management is important here because you need to become familiar with the environment in which your programs execute. Certainly, this information is essential if you advance to more sophisticated levels of programming and begin calling your own shots as to where the program is loaded, how much memory should be allocated, whether your program will load and execute another program (a "child" process), and so on; since you are not there yet, you can confine yourself to a few of the basics.

For application programs, a maximum of 640K of this space is made available. Using some of the currently available expanded memory boards, the technology exists to break the memory barrier; however, DOS is not yet capable of addressing that much memory.

Of this 640K of space, DOS takes up approximately 30K in the low RAM (Random Access Memory) area even before it displays the "A" prompt. This 30K is occupied by the IBMBIO.COM and IBMDOS.COM files. COMMAND.COM, in contrast, resides in high-level memory.

When you enter an external command such as a program name, DOS allocates the largest available block of memory to the program, starting with the first available byte in low-level memory. The first 256 bytes of this memory block are reserved for a control block known as the **Program Segment Prefix** (or **PSP**).

A **control block** refers here to a section of memory that DOS sets aside to store information to which it refers for all subsequent functions. For programs and memory management, this control block is the PSP. For file management functions, this block is the **File Control Block** (or **FCB**) discussed later in this chapter.

Information available in the PSP (constructed by DOS when a program is loaded into memory) is useful to assembly language programmers because they must manage many of the tasks that the Turbo Pascal compiler performs for them.

For example, the original buffer for disk file I/O, referred to as the **Disk Transfer Area** (or **DTA**), is located at offset 80H in the PSP. The DTA is discussed later in this chapter in the section on file management. Similarly, if characters are entered after the program name on the DOS command line, these characters are available at offset 81H (also the DTA) with the total number of parameters appearing in the byte at 80H. If a particular program expects parameters entered at the command line, it can look for them in this area. In the earlier versions of Turbo Pascal, this was the only way to read command line parameters; however, the new releases of Turbo Pascal (beginning with 3.0) provide two useful functions in this regard:

- **ParamStr**(N) returns the Nth parameter from the command line; each parameter is separated by spaces.
- **ParamCount** returns the number of parameters passed to the program in the command line.

In addition to these functions, Turbo also lets you enter command line parameters in the compiler-editor environment, which allows you to test your programs without having to exit the compiler.

To enter command line parameters into a program, select option O from the main compiler menu, followed by P (for parameters). The compiler then prompts you for parameters. You can enter several parameters by separating them with spaces or tabs.

Examples of parameters that programs usually expect are input and output file names, which also include drive and directory path specifiers, and program switches that can influence the execution of a program based on the switches used. For example, you can use DOS's CHKDSK.COM program to list all the files on disk by using this switch:

```
CHKDSK /V
```

Similarly, the FORMAT.COM program accepts a drive letter to specify the drive containing the diskette to be formatted.

In each of these cases, the program extends its usefulness and flexibility by allowing command line parameters to be entered when it is invoked.

Another useful parameter in the PSP is the available memory. This parameter provides another way to obtain the available memory without having to invoke an external subroutine (in this case, an interrupt service routine).

Finally, PSP is the area in which DOS saves the old addresses for the Terminate, CTRL-Break, and Critical Error Handler interrupt services. When a program terminates, these addresses are restored to their original values. This is especially useful for programs that call, load, and execute other programs that may (in the course of execution) alter these addresses. Upon termination of the "child" process, the "parent" program can resume processing in its original environment.

A more detailed picture of the PSP is available in the *DOS Technical Reference Manual.*

DOS Disk File Management

Two aspects of disk file management in PC-DOS will be discussed next:

- disk format
- data allocation

DOS functions available to applications for performing various file management tasks will also be presented.

Disk Format and Data Allocation

A special version of DOS (version 3.2) is available to support IBM's 3-1/2-inch mini diskettes. All future versions of DOS will offer support for this new diskette size.

The introduction of these mini floppy diskettes for the PC family only widens the range of diskette formats available to both users and software developers, from the single-sided, single-density (160K storage capacity) diskette format introduced with the early PCs to the most recent introduction of the high-density, 1.2-megabyte diskette format requiring a special disk drive (available for the PC AT). For serious applications, most programmers must concern themselves with all available formats.

This book only focuses on the most common format: the currently standard 5-1/4-inch, double-sided, double-density diskette with storage capacity of 360K with DOS 2.0 and higher. This diskette provides a good model to show how DOS formats a diskette and allocates data.

As was noted earlier, DOS is responsible for disk formatting and data allocation and will automatically determine the format in use whether you are using a diskette drive, a fixed disk, a standard or high-density diskette, or other disk format. Unless you are writing disk-intensive applications, such as copy-protection schemes or disk formatting and copying utilities, you can use DOS's built-in facilities for performing input/output to the disk drive.

Diskette Structure

Terms such as **tracks** and **sectors** are frequently encountered in the context of disk formats. These terms describe the way DOS divides a disk into small segments, each capable of storing a fixed amount of data. There are two sides to a diskette, numbered 0 and 1. Tracks are concentric circles on each side, ranging from 0 (innermost) to 39 (on the periphery). Each track is divided further into equal "slices" or sectors. While BIOS allows each sector to be 128, 256, 512, or 1024 bytes in size, DOS currently uses only 512-byte sectors. On a standard floppy diskette, there are a total of 720 sectors and 720×512 (or 368,640) bytes of total storage space.

Evidence of other sector sizes is available with DOS's VDISK.SYS—a program that simulates a disk drive in RAM—which supports most of the above sector sizes. VDISK.SYS is loaded as a device driver through the CONFIG.SYS file.

For convenience, DOS numbers all of the sectors on the diskette sequentially, starting with the sectors on track 0 of side 0, followed by sectors on the same track of side 1, and so on.

Floppy diskettes are commonly referred to as **soft-sectored**, a term implying that the diskette is formatted under software (DOS) control. This provides DOS and other programs with flexibility in reading from and writing to a variety of formats, both commercial and proprietary.

Diskette Organization

As a result of the formatting process, DOS segments the diskette into four areas:

- boot record
- file allocation table (two copies)
- directory
- file data area

The **boot record** is always on side 0, track 0, sector 1. In DOS's notation, this is the first sector of the diskette. When the system is powered up or rebooted, BIOS checks this area to ensure that the diskette is DOS-formatted and proceeds to load the boot record into memory. The sequence of instructions in the boot record (if you care to peek using DOS's Debug program) seeks the presence of IBMBIO.COM and IBMDOS.COM files (discussed earlier in this chapter), which should be the first two files on the disk. Initialization proceeds to load each of these files and subsequently transfers control to the control program, COMMAND.COM.

File Allocation Table (FAT)

The **File Allocation Table** (or **FAT**) is used by DOS during disk read and write operations to allocate and search for individual sectors of a file. The FAT occupies two sectors on a standard diskette, and a duplicate copy is provided to preserve integrity. Since the FAT provides DOS with a map of the disk space and file allocation, any corruption of this table can result in loss of data—a situation that usually results in a frantic dash for file recovery utility programs.

You must understand the FAT's organization because you will rely heavily on DOS services (especially interrupts 25H and 26H) and use assembly language routines to perform file I/Os in your Turbo Pascal programs. More information about the FAT and other disk format topics is available in the Appendix of your *DOS Technical Reference Manual.*

Each file on disk is stored in **clusters**, each cluster consisting of two sectors on the standard floppy diskette. The File Allocation Table consists of a 12-bit (1.5-byte) entry for each cluster on disk, specifying whether a cluster is unused and available (000), reserved (hex FF0-FF7), marked as bad (hex FF7), last cluster of a file (hex FF8-FFF), or next cluster of file (hex XXX—any other number between 002 and hex FF0).

The **directory table**, discussed next, contains the first cluster number used by a specific file. Subsequent cluster numbers are derived from the FAT by performing specific calculations provided in the DOS manual. Needless to say, not only can you determine the next cluster of the file, but you can also calculate the relative number of sectors in each cluster as per DOS's conventions. For hackers, this information is valuable because it provides direct access to data on the disk without relying on DOS to read the entire file into memory.

Since DOS allocates disk space for files one cluster at a time—and on a standard floppy diskette a cluster is two 512-byte sectors—what is the minimum space allocated to a file on a standard floppy?

The Directory

The **directory** (root) is created as a result of the formatting process to hold basic information about files stored on disk, such as file name (bytes 0-7), extension (8-10), attribute (11), time of creation (22-23), date of creation (24-25), starting cluster number of the first cluster (26-27), and file size in bytes (28-31).

After obtaining the starting cluster number for a specific file from the directory, you can trace the subsequent clusters from the information provided in the FAT, as discussed earlier.

Note that it is unwise to directly access the FAT or the directory entries since DOS provides many functions to perform most of the common operations; however, this information is presented to help you understand the basic environment in which programs and data are shared between disk and memory. If you want more details, refer to the technical reference manuals for both the computer and DOS.

File Data Area

DOS allocates file space (as needed) one cluster at a time. This implies that on standard floppy diskettes, a file is allocated 1K of data space at a time until the entire file is stored. A 3.2K file will, therefore, actually occupy 4K on disk. It also implies that each file is stored in contiguous clusters, although with subsequent changes in size, a file may eventually end up distributed all over the disk.

If you use the same diskette over and over again to update files, especially data files that may frequently change in size, you will notice a slack in file I/O operations. This is primarily because individual clusters in a file are no longer contiguous, causing the drive head to move longer distances to locate all clusters belonging to a file—a condition that also results in a lot of grinding noise during disk operations. The solution usually involves formatting another disk and copying files to it one at a time until all files are contiguously stored.

DOS Functions

DOS provides application programs with convenient means of file I/O through services accessed via interrupt 21H. Depending on the version of DOS in use, these services range in number from as many as 46 in DOS 1.xx to 98 in DOS 3.1 and perhaps more in the future versions. In addition to providing convenience for programmers, these services are also slowly removing users from low-level access to system resources (especially BIOS services), assuring compatibility with future versions of DOS and newer members of the PC family.

DOS file management functions can be divided into two principal categories: traditional file I/O functions and extended file I/O functions. Details on these and other DOS functions are covered in the *DOS Technical Reference Manual.*

The traditional functions (0DH-24H) introduced with DOS 1.0 perform file I/O using a data structure known as the **File Control Block** (or **FCB**). The FCB stores information such as the drive number, file name and extension, date of creation, file size, record size, and so on. Every file action in this group of functions refers to the FCB of that file. Depending on whether access to individual records within a file is sequential or random, DOS uses the FCB to obtain pertinent information such as the current block and record size to calculate the appropriate cluster on disk for update/retrieval.

A detailed structure of the FCB is presented in the Appendix of the *DOS Technical Reference manual.*

Recent releases of DOS have downplayed the use of FCBs (and, consequently, the functions that rely on them) in favor of the extended functions (39H-57H). These new functions have taken most of the control of file access away from the program and replaced it with a 16-bit identifier referred to as a **file handle**. This number is used internally by DOS to identify the file on which you request specific operations. Rather than having a data structure that you can easily manipulate, you end up with a number. Five of these handles are predefined in DOS and need not be opened before use:

- 0—Std. input device (Turbo's logical device INP:)
- 1—Std. output device (Turbo's logical device OUT:)
- 2—Std. error output (Turbo's logical device ERR:)
- 3—Std. aux. device
- 4—Std. printer device

These predefined handles can be assigned to any file.

A significant advantage of the extended function call is that, unlike FCBs, they allow you to change the current directory between file accesses without influencing a particular read/write operation. With FCBs, you are restricted to maintaining the current directory of the drive specified in the FCB. Clearly, FCBs present a serious limitation, especially to applications developed for fixed-disk users (who are becoming more and more common as the prices of fixed disks approach those of the now-outdated, single-sided drives introduced with the first models of the PC).

You can now begin to consider programming considerations in Turbo Pascal for accessing DOS's memory and disk file management facilities.

A few examples of DOS's memory and disk file management services are provided here as subroutines that can be used in your programs

Function GetCurrDrive

Function GetCurrDrive uses DOS function 19H to determine the current drive. The drive number (0,1,2,...) s returned in the AL register. Following the return, the number is translated into an alpha letter via the XLAT instruction which operates against the string constant Table.

Instead of using the translate table, you can also perform the same operation using the following instruction:

```
add  AL,'A'
```

The function result is returned as a Turbo Pascal character data type. Because the function has no parameters, the result will be four bytes off of the address in BP.

```
Function GetCurrDrive:char;
const
  Table : string[5] = 'ABCDE';
begin
Inline(
  $BB/>TABLE+1      {        mov BX,<TABLE+1      ;set up pointer to TABLE}
  /$B4/$19          {        mov AH,$19           ;DOS service (Current Disk)}
  /$CD/$21          {        int $21              ;Interrupt 21H}
  /$2E/$D7          {     CS:xlat                 ;translate into drive char}
  /$88/$46/<4       {        mov [BP+<4],AL       ;get drive letter}
);
end;
```

```
Program Use

begin
    Write(GetCurrDrive);
end.
```

Get Disk Free Space

Function FreeSpace uses DOS function 36H to determine the available space in Kbytes in the default (@) or specified drive.

On return from the function service routine, the register assignments are as follows:

BX = Clusters
CX = Bytes/Sector
AX = Sectors/Cluster

Free disk space is calculated using the following formula:

```
Avail. Clusters * Sectors/Cluster * Bytes/Sector
```

The result is further modified by 1024 bytes/Kbyte to get the final result in 16-bit representable form.

If the wrong drive is specified, the function returns a -1 ($FFFF returned from DOS as an indication of error). Use Function 59H for additional error detail.

```
Function FreeSpace(Drive:char):integer;
begin
Inline(
  $B4/$36               {          mov AH,$36           ;DOS service (Disk
Free Space)}
  /$8A/$56/<DRIVE       {          mov DL,<Drive[BP]    ;drive letter}
  /$80/$EA/$40          {          sub DL,'@'           ;convert it into
number}
  /$CD/$21              {          int $21              ;Interrupt 21H}
  /$3D/$FF/$FF          {          cmp AX,$FFFF         ;error in drive
letter}
  /$74/$09              {          je  DONE             ;quit}
  /$F7/$E3              {          mul BX               ;clusters *
sectors/cluster}
  /$F7/$E1              {          mul CX               ;sectors *
bytes/sector}
  /$BB/$00/$04          {          mov BX,$400          ;Kbytes}
  /$F7/$F3              {          div BX}
  /$89/$86/>6           {   DONE:  mov [BP+>6],AX       ;get free space}
);
end;
```

Function Set DTA

Function SetDTA uses DOS function 1AH to set a new address for the Disk Transfer Area (DTA), which normally defaults to offset 80H in the PSP (Program Segment Prefix)

On entry, the function contains the address of the new DTA. In the example, this DTA has been set up as a buffer overlaying a record that provides more detailed information about the file being accessed. This data type definition is simply a recommendation. Your application needs may differ.

```
type
   DTABuf   = array[1..128] of byte;

var
  FileInfo : record          { store file information acquired     }
                             { during search                        }
               Filler1   : array[1..21] of byte;
                   Attr  : byte;          { attribute byte          }
                   Time  : integer;
                   Date  : integer;
                  SizLo  : integer;      { size is returned in 4 }
                  SizHi  : integer;      { bytes                  }
                   Name  : array[1..12] of char;
               Filler2   : byte;
             end;

  Buffer  : DTABuf absolute FileInfo;  { a new location for DTA    }
                                        { overlaying atop FileInfo }

Procedure SetDTA(var NewDTA:DTABuf);

begin
Inline(
  $1E                  {  push DS              ;save DS}
  /$C5/$B6/>NewDTA     {  lds  SI,>NewDTA[BP]  ;set pointer to input string}
  /$89/$F2             {  mov  DX,SI           ;set up DS:DX to point to DTA}
  /$B4/$1A             {  mov  AH,$1A          ;request Function 1A (Set DTA)}
  /$CD/$21             {  int  $21             ;}
  /$1F                 {  pop  DS              ;restore DS}
);
end;
```

CHAPTER 12

PROGRAMMING VIDEO DISPLAY–TEXT MODE

Programming video displays is among the most interesting and challenging aspects of software development because most users perceive the display as their sole interface with the application. Regardless of the sophisticated techniques you use to store a file on disk, search a table, or sort a database, they are all transparent to you. The only aspect of video displays you may notice is the overall speed and efficiency with which the software handles operations.

Actually, the display is an important user interface. The display of information, the position of text, the speed with which text is displayed, and the attributes used to display important fields on the screen are all important factors to software developers as well as users.

Programming video displays is challenging because it is through screen displays that the software must convey its user-friendliness and be as informative as possible. To program displays for the various types of display adapters, however, a software developer must understand many technical aspects of video display programming.

This chapter discusses techniques you can use to create and manipulate displays on the monitor screen using Turbo Pascal's built-in subroutines, BIOS and DOS interrupt services, and Inline machine code.

The focus of this chapter is on the text display mode using both the **Monochrome Display Adapter (MDA)** and the **Color Graphics Adapter (CGA)**. These adapters are IBM products, but the techniques should work just as well with compatibles. Chapter 13 will focus on the various graphics modes associated with the CGA.

DISPLAY MODES

The Monochrome Display Adapter is only capable of displaying text and limited graphics (using only the block graphics symbols from the IBM PC's extended ASCII set).

The Color Graphics Display Adapter can display text as well as graphics. It features several graphics modes in low, medium, and high resolution and offers 16 possible text/background color combinations.

The MDA produces text in an 80×25 format, with each character in a 7×9 matrix within a 9×14 cell to allow for underlining. The MDA features a display resolution of 720 horizontal and 350 vertical dots per inch, which is far superior to the resolution of the CGA.

In the text mode, the CGA produces text in an 80×25 format, although the character matrix is only 7×7 in an 8×8 cell. You can also display text in the 40 column mode (40×25 format). You can use up to sixteen foreground colors per character, eight background colors per character, and sixteen border colors.

In the graphics mode, the Color/Graphics Adapter offers medium-resolution graphics of 320 horizontal and 200 vertical dots per inch and high-resolution graphics of 640 horizontal and 200 vertical dots per inch. You can use up to sixteen background and foreground colors in low-resolution and up to sixteen background and four foreground colors in medium-resolution graphics modes. The high-resolution graphics mode, however, offers only black and white for foreground and background.

MEMORY MAPPING

The information displayed on the screen is read directly from a **display buffer**. The screen can be viewed as a 2000-character (80×25) string. At the end of each line, the information is automatically wrapped around to the beginning of the next line. The CRT controller monitors the row and column positions where a character is to be displayed.

Video display generated by mapping the system memory is referred to as **memory-mapped**. Information is written to the screen buffer by the operating system or your program and is continuously moved to the display screen by the CRT controller. Because the display buffer is part of the PC's memory, it can be addressed directly by a program or indirectly through PC-DOS functions and ROM-BIOS services.

Display Buffers

The Monochrome Adapter uses 4K of display memory, starting at location B0000. Because the screen can hold 2000 characters, and each character requires an attribute byte, 4K is enough space for one full screen of display.

The Color/Graphics Adapter uses 16K of memory, starting at location B8000, which is enough space for four screens of information in the 80×25 character display mode. Each screen is referred to as a **page**, and you can direct output to any one of these pages; however, in Turbo Pascal, standard video I/O is always directed to page 0—the default page. To access other pages, you must use ROM BIOS video services. The large memory allocation for this adapter is necessary because the high-resolution graphics mode requires 16K of memory for a single screen of data.

CHARACTER ATTRIBUTES

Each character in the display buffer has a corresponding **attribute** byte, which provides specific information about how the character is to be displayed on the screen. As each character is read from the display buffer, its attribute byte is read and decoded. The value in this byte determines the signals sent to the monitor for each character.

As shown in Figure 12.1, the individual bits of the attribute byte for both the Monochrome and Color Display Adapters are organized in two areas. Bits 0-3 and 7 control the attributes of the foreground, and bits 4-6 control the attributes of the background. Notice that in both adapters, bits 3 and 7 control the foreground intensity and blink attributes respectively, which gives a degree of compatibility to the two adapters; however, the display of each adapter is quite different.

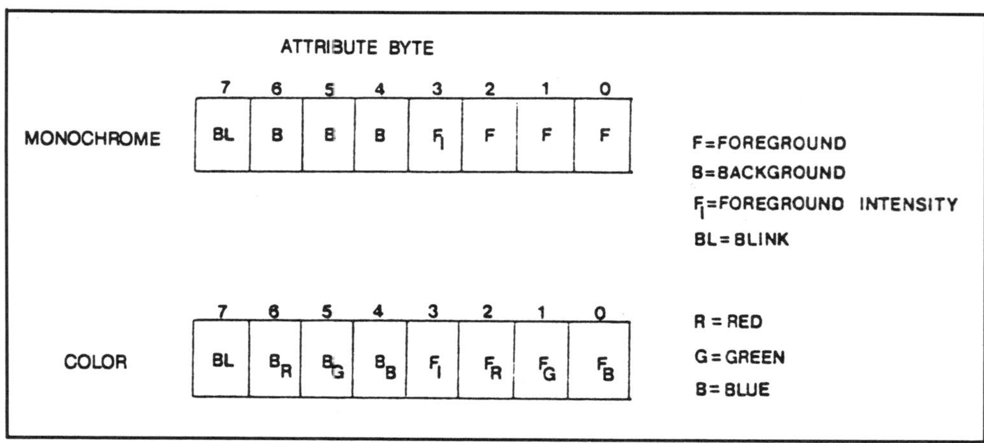

Figure 12.1 Attribute Bytes for Monochrome Display Adaptor and Color Graphics Adaptor

In the context of character display attributes, **foreground** represents the dot pattern of the character to be displayed, and **background** represents the remaining cell area in an 8×8 matrix for color display or 9×14 matrix for monochrome display.

Table 12.1 lists the bit patterns of various character attributes for the two adapters. For more information, refer to *The IBM PC Technical Reference Manual.*

Table 12.1 Character Attribute Bit Patterns

Monochrome Display:

FUNCTION	BITS	7	6	5	4	3	2	1	0	VALUE
Normal		0	0	0	0	0	1	1	1	7
Reverse		0	1	1	1	0	0	0	0	112
Underline		0	0	0	0	0	0	0	1	1
Non-Display		0	0	0	0	0	0	0	0	0

Color Display:

FUNCTION	BITS	7	6	5	4	3	2	1	0	VALUE
			R	G	B		R	G	B	
Normal		0	0	0	0	0	1	1	1	7
Reverse		0	1	1	1	0	0	0	0	112
Non-Display (wht)		0	1	1	1	0	1	1	1	119
Non-Display (blk)		0	0	0	0	0	0	0	0	0

Color Display

Color display values correspond to white characters on a black background; however, you can specify various color combinations for text foreground and background by selectively turning the individual color bits on and off. Turning all three bits (Red, Green, and Blue) "on" will result in white, and turning all three bits "off" will result in black. Turning only one of the three bits "on" will result in the assigned color.

Monochrome and Color Display

To add "blink" to the above values, turn bit 7 on and add 128 to the byte value.

To add intensity to the display, turn bit 3 on and add 8 to the corresponding byte value.

In the display buffer, the character code must be an even address, and the attribute code must be an odd address. Based on the correspondence between the characters in the display buffer and their positions on the screen, you can calculate the position from the row and column where the character is to be placed. The formula is as follows:

CharacterPos = 80 x (Row-1) + 2 x (Column-1)

Similarly, the position of the attribute byte is

AttributeByte = CharacterPos + 1

BIOS SERVICES

BIOS provides many useful services for manipulating the IBM PC's video display (see Table 12.2). These services are accessible directly from Turbo Pascal through the **Intr** procedure as well as through Inline machine code. Many of these services are also available as special built-in procedures in the IBM PC version of Turbo Pascal.

Software interrupt 10H provides access to BIOS video services. Each service or function is called by placing the appropriate value (service number in Table 12.1) in the AH register. Some services also require other parameters via other registers. For more details, see the *IBM PC Technical Reference Manual.*

According to the manual, interrupt 10H restores the CS, SS, DS, ES, BX, CX, and DX registers; however, from the assembly listing in the manual, it also appears to save and restore SI and DI registers, leaving only the BP register for you to consider.

To call interrupt 10H services in Inline code, PUSH and POP BP before and after the INT instruction:

```
push BP
int 10H
pop BP
```

Table 12.2 BIOS Video Services (Interrupt 10H)

SERVICE NO.	FUNCTION
General Display Functions:	
0	Set display mode (40/80-column; Color/BW/Monochrome)
1	Set cursor type (width)
2	Set cursor position (Row/Column; Page number)
3	Read cursor position (Row/Column; Width)
4	Read light pen position
5	Select active display page (CGA text mode only)
6	Scroll active page up
7	Scroll active page down
Character Display Functions:	
8	Read character/attribute at curr. cursor position
9	Write character/attribute at curr. cursor position
10	Write character only at curr. cursor position
Graphics Functions (covered in Chapter 13):	
11	Set color palette
12	Write dot (Row, Column, and Color value)
13	Read dot (Row, Column, and Color value)
ASCII Character Output Function:	
14	Write character to screen
Current Video State Function:	
15	Get current video state (display mode, column width, and active display page)

ROM-BIOS also maintains video display status information in the low-memory area, starting at location 449H. You can access status information provided in this area to determine, for example, the type of display adapter being used or the video display mode.

The following section contains example programs illustrating the use of Inline machine code as well as BIOS services to create and manipulate video display on the IBM PC. For a general discussion of BIOS service, see Chapter 10.

SETTING CURSOR TYPE

In normal text mode, the cursor appears as two blinking scan lines at positions 6 and 7 in the Color Graphics Adapter and positions 12 and 13 in the Monochrome Adapter because the CGA features an 8×8 character matrix, and the MA features a 9×13 matrix.

You can change the position of the cursor within this matrix for either of the two adapters by altering the low and high scan lines through service 1 of Interrupt 10H.

Also, you can alter the width of the cursor from a single scan line to the full matrix (block-shaped) cursor. For example, if you specify the low and high scan lines as 13 in the Monochrome Adapter, the cursor will appear as a single line at the bottom of the text. If the low scan line is specified as 13 and the high scan line is specified as 0, the cursor will appear block-shaped. This service can also be used to make the cursor disappear by placing an invalid value in the CH register.

Upon entry to the Interrupt routine,

```
AH = 1;
CH, CL = high/low scan line;
```

Program 12.1 illustrates a procedure used to set cursor shape by specifying low and high scan lines. You can enhance this procedure by checking for invalid values for scan lines.

Program 12.1

```
procedure SetCursor(LoScanLine, HiScanLine:byte);
{
 ----------------------------------------------------------
  Sets cursor shape based on the low and high scan lines
  specified.
 ----------------------------------------------------------
}
begin
  InLine(
         $90/$90/$90/
         $B4/$01              {    mov AH,01                 }
        /$8A/$4E/<HiScanLine  {    mov CL,<HiScanLine[BP]    }
        /$8A/$6E/<LoScanLine  {    mov CH,<LoScanLine[BP]    }
        /$55                  {    push BP                   }
        /$CD/$10              {    Int 10                    }
        /$5D                  {    pop BP                    }
       );
end;
```

SETTING CURSOR POSITION

Service 2 of Interrupt 10H is similar to Turbo's GoToXY procedure in that it directs the cursor to the row and column specified on the screen. While GoToXY controls cursor position on page 0, Service 2 can control cursor position on any one of the four (or eight in 40-column mode) active display pages (CGA text mode only).

On entry to Int 10H,

```
AH = 2;
DH,DL = row, column;
BH = page
```

Program 12.2

```
procedure SetCursorPos(Row, Column, Page: Byte);
{
 --------------------------------------------------------------
 Set cursor position be specifying Row, Column, and Active
 Page.
 --------------------------------------------------------------
}
begin
  Inline(
       $B4/$02              {     mov AH,02             }
       /$8A/$76/<ROW        {     mov DH,<Row[BP]       }
       /$8A/$56/<COLUMN     {     mov DL,<Column[BP]    }
       /$8A/$7E/<PAGE       {     mov BH,<Page[BP]      }
       /$55                 {     push BP               }
       /$CD/$10             {     Int 16                }
       /$5D                 {     pop BP                }
         );
end;
```

READ CURSOR POSITION

Service 3 of Interrupt 10H is analogous to Turbo's WhereX and WhereY functions in that it returns the position of the cursor's column and row respectively. It can also be used to find the cursor position of any one of the active display pages and also returns the cursor type (high and low scan lines).

On entry to INT 10H,

```
AH = 3;
BH = page
```

On exit,

```
DH,DL = row, column of cursor;
CH,CL = high, low scan line
```

Program 12.3

```
procedure ReadCursor(var Row, Column, LoScan,HiScan:byte;
                                                 Page:byte);
{
  -------------------------------------------------------------
  Reads cursor position in row and column on specified page.
  Also returns high and low scan lines.
  -------------------------------------------------------------
}
begin
    Inline($90/$90/$90/
           $B4/$03                  {  mov AH,03           }
          /$8A/$7E/<Page            {  mov BH,<Page[BP] }
          /$55                      {  push BP             }
          /$CD/$10                  {  Int 16              }
          /$5D                      {  pop BP              }
          /$88/$76/<Row             {  mov <Row[BP],DH    }
          /$88/$56/<Column          {  mov <Column[BP],DL }
          /$88/$6E/<LoScan          {  mov <LoScanLine[BP],CH }
        /$88/$4E/<HiScan            {  mov <HiScanLine[BP],CL  }
          );
end;
```

BIOS DATA AREA

The video status information in the BIOS data area occupies 30 bytes, starting at locations 449H-466H. Table 12.3 lists the information available in this area and the corresponding addresses.

Table 12.3 Video Display Status Information

ADDRESS (hex)	LENGTH (Bytes)	STATUS
0000:0449	1	Current display mode
0000:044A	2	Number of columns on screen
0000:044C	2	Screen regeneration length
0000:044E	2	Starting address of active page
0000:0450	16	Cursor position for each page
0000:0460	2	Current cursor size
0000:0462	1	Active display page number
0000:0463	2	Port address of CRT Controller
0000:0465	1	Current mode of the 3__8 register
0000:0466	1	Current palette setting

The status information provided at locations in Table 12.3 is accessed by applications and DOS to determine the system configuration and the status of various devices. These locations may be considered as "read only"; however, you may wish to modify values at some of these locations. The modification itself will not always produce changes in the display status, but it can fool a program into thinking that the system is set up differently than it is. Results of such modifications are not guaranteed because programs do not have a standard approach to determining device status, and they may not access this information.

PROGRAMMING THE CRT CONTROLLER

Both the Monochrome and Color Graphics Display Adapters use the Motorola 6845 CRT controller to drive the video display. In the following section, the theory and programming considerations associated with each are discussed.

The 6845 CRT Controller drives the signals that display the contents of the screen buffer. In the text mode, the Controller uses the ASCII value for each character in display memory through the ROM Character Generator to find the bit pattern for that character. The attribute byte is processed through an Attribute Decoder to determine how each character is to be displayed and also to keep track of the row and column positions where each character is to be displayed. In the graphics mode (CGA only), the bit pattern in display memory is directly accessed, and the Character Generator is bypassed.

In both Monochrome and Color Graphics Adapters, access to the CRT Controller is available through I/O ports. These ports are eight-bit registers providing video status information allowing you to change display modes, display a blank screen, select border colors, etc.

Turbo's predefined arrays—**Port** and **PortW** (2 bytes)—can be used to read and write to these ports. Depending on which side of the assignment statement the array is specified, the array will read from or write to the port. For example,

```
const
  Cyan : Integer = 1;

begin
  Port[$3D9] := Cyan;    { select border color }
  .
  .
  .
```

The previous statement will cause the value of the variable "Cyan" to be assigned to the port at address $3D9. This port is the Color Select register on the CGA.

The addresses of the ports are specific for both Monochrome and Color Graphics Display Adapters. For the Monochrome Adapter, the ports are as follows:

CRT Status Port	@ hex 3BA
CRT Control Port	@ hex 3B8
6845 Index register	@ hex 3B4
6845 Address register	@ hex 3B5

The **CRT Status port** is "read only" and provides information on the status of the horizontal sync signal and the video dots going to the monitor.

The **CRT Control port** has three active bits at positions 0, 3, and 5. The low bit turns the high resolution mode "on" and must be set to a "1" before access is made to the adapter to set other values (otherwise, the system will crash). Bit 3 toggles the video on and off. Setting this bit to "0" will cause a blank screen. Bit 5 controls the "blink" attribute of text display.

The 6845 Index and Data registers apply to both monochrome and color display adapters.

The **6845 CRT Controller** contains 18 programmable internal registers controlling various display parameters. Specific details on each register are discussed in the *IBM PC Technical Reference Manual.* Some of these registers (the first ten) are "hands off"; they generate sensitive signals and should not be experimented with. If you are curious about these registers, *Graphics Primer For The IBM PC* contains some experiments you can perform by applying various values to these registers. The remaining registers control the shape of the cursor, its position, display page (CGA), and light pen signals.

The most interesting feature of these registers is how they are accessed. Instead of a port for each register, the CRT Controller provides the 6845 Index register (which holds the number of the programmable register to which you want to output data) and the 6845 Address register (which contains the data you want to output). The Index register serves as a pointer to the other eighteen registers.

In addition to these four ports, the Color Graphics adapter also contains ports for selecting various display modes, screen text, background, and border colors. These ports are as follows:

Mode select	@ hex 3D8
Color select	@ hex 3D9
Status	@ hex 3DA
6845 Index	@ hex 3D4
6845 Addr	@ hex 3D5
Set light pen latch	@ hex 3DC
Clear light pen latch	@ hex 3DB

The Status, Index, and Address registers are similar to the Monochrome Adapter (with the addition of light pen status information).

The **Mode Select** register is "write only" and allows you to select from available text and graphics modes. The most commonly used feature of this register is the "video enable" toggle switch, which presents a solution to the "video snow" problem by disabling the video signal during the write operation. This procedure causes the blinking of the screen you may have observed in word processors and screen graphics programs. Bit 3 of this register controls the video enable signal. The descriptions of Bit 3 and other bits follow:

Bit	ON	OFF
0	80×25 mode	40×25 mode
1	Graphics	Text
2	Color burst disable (B/W)	enable
3	Video "ON"	"OFF"
4	Hi-resolution graphics	
5	Blink disable	enable

The **Color Select** register is also a "write only" register and is frequently accessed for selecting screen border colors or a graphics color palette and adding intensity to text background color.

CHAPTER 13

PROGRAMMING VIDEO DISPLAY—GRAPHICS MODE

Chapter 12 began a discussion of techniques for programming the PC's video display. The focus was the text display mode, which primarily involves displaying the standard ASCII character set with limited block graphics capability. In the process of learning how the PC's video display is generated, several basic concepts were also introduced. As some of those concepts also apply to the graphics display mode (discussed in this chapter), you may want to review the basics of video display in Chapter 12 before proceeding with this chapter.

This chapter concludes the discussion on video display programming by discussing the more challenging and interesting mode of video display—the **graphics mode**. The focus is on the graphics mode available with IBM's Color Graphics Adapter (CGA). The techniques that you learn should work just as well on CGA clones, as long as they are quality clones.

DISPLAY MODES

To quickly recap the CGA's display modes, recall from Chapter 12 that the CGA can display text as well as graphics. It features several graphics modes in low, medium, and high resolution and also offers 16 possible text/background color combinations.

In the low resolution mode, you can access 160×200 dots on the screen. Similarly, the medium resolution graphics mode features 320×200 dots on the screen, and high resolution graphics mode features 640×200 dots on the screen.

Furthermore, you can also have up to sixteen background and foreground colors in low resolution and up to sixteen background and four foreground colors in medium resolution graphics modes. The high resolution graphics mode, however, only offers black and white colors for foreground and background.

MAPPING GRAPHICS DISPLAY MEMORY

Also recall from Chapter 12 that in the text mode, the display consists of a matrix of 2000 characters in 80x25 format, i.e., 80 columns and 25 rows.

The graphics mode is quite similar in design. Instead of characters, however, the graphics mode deals with dots. Specifically, the graphics mode screen is built from a matrix (or grid) of as many as 64,000 dots in medium-resolution mode and 128,000 dots in high-resolution mode. The low-resolution mode is rarely used.

These dots are more commonly referred to as **pixels** (derived from **PIC**ture **EL**ement). A display is produced by turning these pixels on and off, as you will see later in this chapter.

The graphics display in both modes takes up the full 16K of memory; therefore, there is only one display page in graphics modes. Also, graphics memory mapping is done in two 8K banks, the first one storing the even numbered lines and the second one storing the odd numbered lines.

The display buffer for both the text and graphics modes of the Color Graphics Adapter begins at the same address—B8000H. Their sizes differ, since text mode is divided into four pages of 4K each and graphics display mode is a single 16K page, as discussed earlier.

In contrast to the text display mode, in which the character generator generates the text on the screen and all you need to do is supply the ASCII code for the character, the graphics mode gives you the whole screen and all available pixels to generate your own bit patterns, which is one reason why the graphics mode is more challenging.

Each pixel in display memory corresponds to a dot on the screen. In this respect, the display is often referred to as being **bit mapped**. Also, in the same context, all bits are addressable in your programs, i.e., you can address specific bits either directly, through IBM's ROM-BIOS services, or through Turbo's predefined functions and procedures. The phrase **all points addressable** (APA) is also used to describe this concept.

COLOR PALETTES

In the medium resolution graphics modes, you have a choice of four foreground colors and up to 16 background colors. These four colors are available in color palettes of which there are four. (Actually, there are only two color palettes documented. The other two are the high-intensity versions of the first two.) Only one palette may be used on a screen at one time, and when you change the palette selection, all the colors on the screen change to colors corresponding to the new palette, so you cannot mix palettes.

Your *Turbo Pascal User Reference Manual* has the various color palettes and corresponding numbers presented in Table 19-3.

The high-resolution mode only offers one foreground color, and that may be one of sixteen available colors (or eight if your monitor cannot display the high intensity version of these colors).

BIOS GRAPHICS SERVICES VIA INT 10H

The PC's BIOS provides a limited number of services to support graphics display programming. These services are available via Interrupt 10H. They are basic services that you can include in your routines to develop various graphics subroutines.

This section provides a brief discussion of these services, with examples of routines in assembly language. Once you begin writing graphics routines in assembly language (preferably Inline machine code), you will realize that the principal advantage of interfacing assembly language with Turbo Pascal is speed, which is not to take anything away from Turbo's built-in routines for graphics, as they are also relatively fast.

As stated earlier, interrupt 10H provides access to BIOS video services. Each service or function is called by putting the appropriate value (service number in Table 10.3—see Chapter 10) in the AH register. Some services also require other parameters via other registers. These parameters will be discussed in the context of the specific service.

It is clear that the BIOS services do not offer any significant advantage over the subroutines available in Turbo Pascal, especially in the extended graphics mode; however, once you understand how to invoke these services in Turbo Pascal programs, you will be at ease with other graphics adapters, such as the **Enhanced Graphics Adapter** (EGA), which Turbo currently does not support, but it is soon to become the industry standard.

The BIOS services for the graphics mode are described next.

Service 11—Set Color Palette

This service, similar to Turbo's graphics procedure Palette, selects one of the available palettes in the medium resolution graphics mode.

On entry to Int 10H,

AH = 11
BH = palette color ID
BL = color value

```
Procedure Palette(Palette, Color: byte);
{
 -----------------------------------------------------------------------
 Set color palette

 On entry  AH = 11;  BH = Palette color ID;  BL = Color value
 -----------------------------------------------------------------------
}
begin
Inline(
  $B4/$0B              {    mov AH,$0B            ;requesting service 11}
  /$8A/$7E/<PALETTE    {    mov BH,<Palette[BP]   ;palette color ID}
  /$8A/$5E/<COLOR      {    mov BL,<Color[BP]     ;color value}
  /$55                 {    push BP               ;save BP}
  /$CD/$10             {    Int $10               ;invole BIOS video service}
  /$5D                 {    pop BP                ;restore BP}
);
end;  { procedure Palette }
```

Service 12—Write Dot

This service, similar to Turbo's graphics procedure Plot, writes a dot (or plots a point) at the specified coordinates on the screen.

On entry to Int 10H,

AH = 12
DL = row number
CX = column number

```
Procedure WriteDot(Column:integer;Row,Color:byte);
{
 -----------------------------------------------------------------------
 Plot a point on the screen

 On entry  AH = 12; DL = Y coord;  CX = X coord;  AL = color
 -----------------------------------------------------------------------
}

begin
Inline(
  $B4/$0C                 {     mov AH,$0C             ;requesting service 12}
  /$8A/$56/<ROW           {     mov DL,<Row[BP]        ;row}
  /$8B/$8E/>COLUMN        {     mov CX,>Column[BP]     ;column}
  /$8A/$46/<COLOR         {     mov AL,<Color[BP]      ;color value}
  /$55                    {     push BP                ;save BP}
  /$CD/$10                {     Int $10                ;invole BIOS video service}
  /$5D                    {     pop BP                 ;restore BP}
);
end;  { procedure WriteDot}
```

Service 13—Read Dot

This service, similar to Turbo's graphics function GetDotColor, gets the color value of a dot at the specified coordinates on the screen.

On entry to Int 10H,

AH = 13
DL = row number
CX = column number

On exit,

AL = the pixel value (the color attribute)

```
Function ReadDot(Row:byte;Column:integer):byte;
{
 ---------------------------------------------------------------------
 Reads a dot on the screen

 On entry  AH = 12; DL = Y coord;  CX = X coord;
 On exit   AL = dot color
 ---------------------------------------------------------------------
}

begin
Inline(
  $B4/$0D              {    mov AH,$0D              ;requesting service 13}
  /$8A/$56/<ROW        {    mov DL,<Row[BP]         ;pixel row}
  /$8B/$8E/>COLUMN     {    mov CX,>Column[BP]      ;pixel column}
  /$55                 {    push BP                 ;save BP}
  /$CD/$10             {    Int $10                 ;invoke BIOS video service}
  /$5D                 {    pop BP                  ;restore BP}
  /$88/$46/<$08        {    mov [BP+<$08],AL        ;set function result}
);

end;  { procedure ReadDot }
```

CHAPTER 14

READING KEYBOARD INPUT

To effectively interface with users, an application must be responsive to user input via the primary input device—the keyboard. The application must be able to keep up with users (including lightning-fast typists), distinguish between various special key combinations, quickly detect data-entry errors, allow command and macro input via special function keys, and allow keyboard customization for specific needs. Combining these features in an application requires programming special routines to read keyboard input.

Programming the PC's keyboard is a challenge because of the various ways to use edit control keys, programmable function keys, and numerous key combinations with the Shift, Alt, and Ctrl keys.

Each key on the keyboard has a special code (scan code) associated with it. When you press a key, the keyboard microprocessor sends the scan code to the PC. The BIOS and DOS keyboard services translate this code into the corresponding ASCII code for DOS and application programs; however, for control over keyboard input, low-level interfaces often read these scan codes directly in your programs.

This control is necessary in applications that associate function keys with pop-up screens. For example, you may want to write an application in which function key F1 is the Help key so that when you press the F1 key, a pop-up help window appears. To incorporate this into your program, you must monitor the code for each key entered at the keyboard, intercept the F1 key, and transfer control to the pop-up screen routine.

Similarly, a combination of Ctrl-Alpha keys can be used to activate special commands. Again, monitoring keyboard input is required. The basic theory and examples of these techniques are presented later.

This chapter covers the basics of keyboard input and presents examples of low-level interface you can write in Turbo Pascal programs using Inline machine code and BIOS and DOS services.

To understand the keyboard input mechanism, you must focus on two primary areas:

- what takes place when a key is pressed
- how a program recognizes what key is pressed and when the key is pressed

Familiarity with keyboard operation will enhance your understanding of keyboard input techniques and will help you design your own routines for specific applications.

KEYBOARD BASICS

The PC keyboard has a "brain" of its own—the **8048 microprocessor** located inside the keyboard itself. This processor, or **Keyboard Controller**, detects when a key is pressed and released and reports this information to the 8088 processor. So that a program can identify which key is pressed or released, each key is assigned a unique code (**scan code**) when it is pressed and a different code when it is released. These two codes may be read by a program (through the BIOS keyboard routines that translate codes into corresponding ASCII values) or directly with the program itself managing the translation. Most applications use the BIOS keyboard services for reading keyboard scan codes.

When a key is pressed, the keyboard controller sends a hardware interrupt signal to the 8088. The interrupt is eventually serviced by the interrupt 9H service routines. Interrupt 9H ISR (interrupt service routine) reads the scan codes for each signal and translates them into corresponding ASCII values.

The INT 9 service routine reads the scan code at port 60 (hex) and translates it into two bytes of data, the low byte containing the ASCII value (in hex) corresponding to the key (if it was one of the ASCII characters) and the high byte containing the scan code (also in hex). These two bytes are placed in a 32-byte circular buffer at hex 41E.

If the key is one of the shift keys (Shift, Ctrl, or Alt) or one of the toggle keys (Scroll Lock, Num Lock), the current shift or toggle state is updated at locations hex 417 and 418 in low memory (the keyboard data area), and no codes are generated for the keyboard buffer.

Because the keyboard contains 83 keys, there are 83 possible scan codes to indicate a "key-pressed" condition and 83 codes to indicate a "key-released" condition. The latter conditions are generated by turning "on" the high bit of the key-pressed scan code byte; therefore, the "key-released" scan code for a key is hex 80 (or 128) greater than the "key-pressed" code.

The "key-released" scan codes are usually ignored in programs because the release of keys is not significant to most applications.

The PC's programmable function keys and cursor control keys are special cases for scan codes. When one of these keys is pressed, the INT 9 routine returns a 0 value in the low byte (ASCII code) and the scan code in the high byte; therefore, a program expecting a special key input must look at the scan code to determine what key was pressed.

The *IBM PC Technical Reference Manual* contains a complete listing of various key combinations and their corresponding scan codes. The *Turbo Pascal User Reference Manual* also contains a table of "keyboard return codes," i.e., scan codes recognized by Turbo Pascal.

KEYBOARD DATA AREA

As mentioned earlier, the INT 9 routine does not translate the scan codes for the Shift, Ctrl, and Alt keys or the toggle keys (Num Lock and Scroll Lock). The routine reports their current state to a special area in low memory called the **keyboard data area**, which is a part of the BIOS keyboard data area. The first two bytes of this data area contain individual bits or flags corresponding to specific keys, as shown in Table 14.1.

For each bit position in Table 14.1, a "1" indicates that the corresponding key is active. For example, the low bit of the first byte is a "1" if the right Shift key is depressed.

Table 14.1 lists the flags associated with the various bit positions in the two bytes in the keyboard data areas.

Table 14.1 Bit Flags In First Two Bytes Of Keyboard Status

BIT POS.	FLAG
Byte 1	
7	Insert State Active
6	Caps Lock Toggled
5	Num Lock Toggled
4	Scroll Lock Toggled
3	Alt Key Depressed
2	Ctrl Key Depressed
1	Left Shift Key Depressed
0	Right Shift Key Depressed
Byte 2	
7	Insert Key Depressed
6	Caps Lock Depressed
5	Num Lock Depressed
4	Scroll Lock Depressed
3	Suspend Key Toggled
2	-- undocumented --
1	-- undocumented --
0	-- undocumented --

DOS handles most of these flag settings for normal data input. For example, you needn't monitor the Caps Lock key in your program because DOS monitors it and prints uppercase alpha characters whenever this key is toggled "on" or activated. You may, however, want to monitor these flags if you are designing custom key-input routines.

The keyboard data area also contains a 32-byte buffer, which begins at locations hex 41E-43E. INT 9 stores input characters and scan codes in this buffer for the operating system and application programs.

To expand the size of this buffer, you can change both its address and length. Later models of the PC have an "extra keyboard data area" at locations hex 480-482. These two bytes can be used to hold the new address of the buffers. After you update these locations with values for a new buffer, you must change the pointer values for the head and tail of the buffer.

BIOS KEYBOARD INTERRUPT 16H

While the service routine for interrupt 9H places input characters in the keyboard buffer, another ISR associated with interrupt 16H is available for reading the character from the buffer.

Depending on the value in the AH register, interrupt 16H offers the following services:

- retrieve the next character from the keyboard buffer (AH=0)
- test for a character in the buffer (AH=1)
- determine current shift status (AH=2)

Retrieve Next Character from Buffer

Service 0 (AH=0) of Interrupt 16H retrieves the first available character from the keyboard buffer. The ASCII code for the character is returned in the AL register, and the scan code is returned in the AH register. For all practical purposes, the character is removed from the buffer.

If a pressed key is an extended key, i.e., one of the special function keys, cursor control keys, or Shift, Alt, and Ctrl keys, the AL register (ASCII value) is returned with a 0; therefore, programs must read the scan code for extended keys in the AH register to identify which key has been pressed.

If the keyboard buffer is empty, the system enters a "wait" state until a key is pressed; therefore, it is recommended that you peek into the buffer (see service 1) to ensure that a character is waiting before using this service to retrieve it, especially if you do not want the program to cease all operations and wait for input.

Program 14.1 reads keyboard input via interrupt 16H and converts the ASCII and scan codes into displayable hexadecimal format for output to the screen.

Program 14.1

```
(* ------------------------------------------------------------ *)
(*                                                   4/10/87     *)
(* Author: Sanjiva Nath                              Version 1   *)
(*                                                               *)
(* Description: Reading keyboard scan codes using Intr 16H.      *)
(* Derived from Ted Mirecki's code in June '84's PC Tech J.      *)
(* ------------------------------------------------------------ *)
Program ScanKey;

type
  Str6 = string[6];
var
   Str : Str6;

Procedure ScanCode(var HexStr:Str6);
const
  Table : string[16] = '0123456789ABCDEF';
begin
Inline($90/$90/$90);
Inline(
  $31/$C9             {       xor CX,CX            ;clear CX}
  /$31/$C0         {GETKEY:   xor AX,AX            ;clear AX}
  /$CD/$16            {       int $16              ;get keyboard input}
                      { AH=scan code AL=ASCII code                     }
  /$80/$FC/$00        {       cmp AH,0            ;is it Ctrl-Break}
  /$74/$31            {       je  QUIT            ;then quit}
  /$C4/$BE/>HEXSTR    {       les DI,[BP+>HEXSTR] ;set up pointer to string}
  /$26/$C6/$05/$06    {    ES:mov [DI],BYTE PTR 6;init string length}
  /$47                {       inc DI              ;bump pointer}
  /$26/$C7/$45/$04/$0D/$24 {ES:mov [DI+4],WORD PTR $240D  ;}
  /$BB/>TABLE+1       {       mov BX,<TABLE+1     ;set up pointer to TABLE}
  /$B1/$04            {       mov CL,4            ;init counter}
  /$D1/$C0         {NEXTNIBL:    rol AX,1         ;rotate left}
  /$D1/$C0            {       rol AX,1            ;four bits}
  /$D1/$C0            {       rol AX,1            ;}
  /$D1/$C0            {       rol AX,1            ;}
  /$89/$C2            {       mov DX,AX           ;save AX}
  /$24/$0F            {       and AL,$0F          ;save lower nibble}
  /$2E/$D7            {    CS:xlat                ;translate}
  /$AA                {       stosb               ;store into string array}
```

continued...

...from previous page

```
  /$89/$D0            {       mov  AX,DX            ;restore AX}
  /$E2/$ED            {       loop NEXTNIBL         ;next nibble}
  /$C4/$56/<HEXSTR    {       les  DX,<HEXSTR[BP]   ;DS:DX point to string}
  /$42                {       inc  DX               ;bump pointer length}
  /$B4/$09            {       mov  AH,9             ;select DOS function 9H}
  /$CD/$21            {       int  $21              ;display string}
  /$EB/$C6            {       jmp  GETKEY           ;get next key}
                      {QUIT                         ;quit}
);

end;

begin
  WriteLn('Press Any Key;  Ctrl-Break to end');
  WriteLn('Codes in hex SSAA format  SS-scan code AA-ASCII code');
  ScanCode(Str);
end.
```

Program 14.1 reads keyboard input using BIOS interrupt 16H. As mentioned earlier, Interrupt 16H places the ASCII and scan codes for a key in the keyboard buffer. Interrupt 16H returns these codes in the AL and AX registers respectively. As you execute the program, note that the program will enter a "wait" state until input from the keyboard is received. This occurs as a result of service 0 of Interrupt 16H, which does not check first to see if the buffer has any characters before attempting to read it.

Procedure ScanCode was initially designed to return in a string or array the two codes for each key pressed (the parameter by reference). Since then, it has been modified to create this crude demonstration. The translation table can be defined as an array; therefore, you needn't worry about the length byte.

Also, the procedure includes code to display the contents of the string containing the ASCII and scan codes. To use the procedure in your program, remove this code since all you need are the two codes determining which key was pressed.

As always, Dave Baldwin's Inline program (see Chapter 7) was used to generate the machine code from the assembly language source.

Peeking into the Keyboard Buffer

Service 1 (AH=1) performs two functions. First, it peeks into the keyboard buffer and informs a program if a character is available by setting the Z flag (bit 6) of the Flag register to a 0 (see the discussion on 8088 registers in Chapter 3 for more detail on the Flag register).

Second, it reports the character in the AX register (ASCII code in AL and scan code in AH). Note the use of the term "report" instead of "retrieve." While the character is presented in the AX register, it remains in the buffer. The next service performing a retrieve on that buffer will also retrieve the same character.

If the "peeking" action of this service sounds familiar, it is because it is also used by Turbo's **KeyPressed** function, which, as you may recall, returns a Boolean value indicating whether or not a character is present in the keyboard buffer. Using this service in your program, therefore, closely simulates the KeyPressed function.

Program 14.2 simulates Turbo's KeyPressed function. The program uses service 2 of Interrupt 16H to check for a "key pressed" condition. This service peeks at the keyboard buffer to see if a character is waiting. In addition to returning the Boolean result, the service also brings back the ASCII or scan code of the key in the buffer. Again, remember that it has not retrieved any character. It simply *reports* the first available character in the buffer.

Because the program checks for "normal" as well as extended keys, you can modify it to return the ASCII and scan codes for both types of keys in a (integer) variable and then determine which routine is to actually retrieve the key and process it.

A 10-second delay is initially set up so you can enter a character in the buffer before the program attempts to peek at it.

Also, you may find it interesting that the function result is returned in BP+8 byte of the stack. This return happens because the function's only parameter is an address of a global variable (passed by reference) occupying four bytes starting at BP+4. Remember, function results are placed on the stack immediately after all the parameters.

Program 14.2

```
Program PeekKbdBuffer;
var
   key:byte;

Function KeyPress(var Inkey:byte):boolean;
begin
 Inline($90/$90/$90);
Inline(
  $31/$DB              {         xor   BX,BX      ;clear register}
  /$B4/$01             {         mov   AH,$01     ;kbd buffer check service}
  /$CD/$16             {         int   $16        ;kbd input service routines}
  /$74/$13             {         jz    NOCHAR     ;Z flag = 1 means no character}
  /$C4/$BE/>INKEY      {         les   DI,[BP+>InKey] ;set up pointer to INKEY}
  /$3C/$00             {         cmp   AL,0       ;Test for extended key}
  /$74/$06             {         je    EXTKEY     ;}
  /$26/$88/$05         {     ES:mov   [DI],AL    ;get ASCII code}
  /$E9/$03/$00         {         jmp   SETFLAG    ;}
  /$26/$88/$25      { EXTKEY: ES:mov   [DI],AH    ;get scan code}
  /$FE/$C3          { SETFLAG:   inc   BL}
  /$88/$9E/>$08     { NOCHAR: mov  [BP+>$08],BL ;set function result}
);
end;

begin
   Key := 0;                                    { initialize key }
   writeLn('You have 10 sec to hit a key');
   delay(1000);                                 { set up delay    }
   If KeyPress(Key) then                        { call function   }
      WriteLn('Key : ',key)
   else
      WriteLn('Nothing in the buffer');
end.
```

Get Current Shift Key Status

Service 2 (AH=2) reports the current status of the shift (Alt, Control, and Left and Right Shift) and toggle keys (Num lock, Scroll lock, Caps Lock, and Insert). This information is returned by turning individual bits corresponding to these keys "on" or "off," depending on the state of the keys. This service is useful for designing programs using special key combinations. For each key pressed, you can use this service to check the state of a particular key before branching to the specific action requested by the user. Because few programs utilize these key combinations, this service is relatively uncommon.

DOS FUNCTIONS

DOS also provides several services or functions for reading keyboard input. While seldom used directly in Turbo Pascal programs, these services will be discussed briefly in the following section.

These functions are accessed through Turbo's **MsDos** procedure. A specific call is made by placing the function number in the AH register (before the register set is passed) as a parameter to the MsDos procedure. Many calls also require specific values in other registers.

Specifically, DOS offers seven functions related to keyboard input:

- Function 1—Keyboard input
- Function 6—Direct keyboard/console I/O
- Function 7—Keyboard input, no echo
- Function 8—Same as 7 with Ctrl/Break checking
- Function 10—Buffered keyboard input
- Function 11—Check keyboard buffer for character
- Function 12—Clear buffer, invoke function 1, 6, 7, or 8

Many of these functions are actually directed at the standard input device—usually the keyboard—unless DOS redirection facilities are used.

Table 14.2 DOS Functions For Keyboard Input

FUNCTION (HEX)	ON ENTRY	DESCRIPTION	INPUT ECHOED	CTRL-C CHECKING
1	AH = 1	Waits for keyboard input Returns character in AL AL = 0 for extended ASCII codes	Yes	Yes
6	AH = 6 DL = FF or DL = Char	If DL = FF, then reads kbd input Returns character in AL and ZF = 0 or no character in AL and ZF = 1. If DL < FF, then Writes out character in DL	No	No
7	AH = 7	Waits for keyboard input	No	No
8	AH = 8 AL = 0	Waits for keyboard input Returns character in AL for extended ASCII codes	No	Yes
A	AH = A	Keyboard input into a buffer DS:DX point to the buffer	No	No
B	AH = B	Checks keyboard buffer for char AL = FF if character is available AL = 0 if no character is available	No	Yes
C	AH = C AL = Fn #	Clears keyboard buffer Executes function in AL		

A brief discussion for each of these functions is provided in the following section. For quick reference, Table 14.2 summarizes these functions and should prove useful for comparing their similarities and differences. Function values are presented in hex unless otherwise indicated. For more details, see the *DOS Technical Reference Manual.*

Note that if keyboard input operation in any of the following functions returns a "0" in AL, an extended key is implied; therefore, you should immediately invoke the read operation a second time to find the scan code for that key.

AH=1 (Keyboard Input)

This function reads a character from the keyboard buffer. The character is returned in the AL register. If no character is available, the function waits for input, which is simultaneously echoed to the screen. This routine also checks for the Ctrl-Break/Ctrl-C keys. DOS interrupt INT 23H is executed when either of those key combinations is encountered.

You can override the INT 23H with your own Ctrl-Break handler, thereby controlling program execution and termination. See Chapter 10 for more details on INT 23H and other DOS interrupts. See Chapter 15 for more details on writing your own Ctrl-Break service routine.

AH=6 (Keyboard/Console I/O)

This function combines keyboard input and character output operations into one package, depending on the value in the DL register.

As indicated in Table 14.2, if the value in DL is hex FF, the function examines the keyboard buffer for character input. If a character is available, it is returned in the AL register with the Z flag set to a "0"; otherwise, the Z flag is set to a "1," and the function returns without character input.

If the value in DL is other than hex FF, it is assumed to be a character that is to be displayed on the screen. No check is made for Ctrl-Break/Ctrl-C key combinations.

One feature of function 6 is that it does not wait for character input. If the buffer is empty, function 6 returns with nothing in the AL register and the Z flag set, in contrast to the other keyboard input routines (Turbo's Read statement, service 0 of INT 16H, and DOS function 1), which usually wait for character input.

This routine is significant for programs that merely check the keyboard for input at some intervals, but do not wait until a key is pressed.

AH=7 (Keyboard Input No Echo)

This function is the same as the Keyboard Input operation of Function 6 except that in the absence of a character in the keyboard buffer, this function waits for input. As emphasized earlier, Function 6 does not wait for character input and merely sets the Z flag if no character is encountered in the buffer. The character input is returned in AL. If AL is zero, a special key is implied; you should make a second call to retrieve the scan code for that key.

Also like Function 6, this function does not perform Ctrl-C checking or echo input on the screen.

AH=8 (Keyboard Input No Echo)

This keyboard input function is similar to function 7 but offers Ctrl-C checking.

AH=10 (Buffered Keyboard Input)

So far, the focus has been on reading keyboard input one character at a time. This particular DOS function allows you to store character input in a buffer. The input is terminated by a carriage return.

The DS:DX register pair must be pointing to the area in memory where input is to be stored. The first byte of this input buffer specifies the number of characters the buffer can store (maximum length), and the second byte specifies how many characters are currently in the buffer. The carriage return terminates input; therefore, it is always the last key read by this function. Also, if more characters are entered than specified in the buffer length, all excessive characters are ignored.

AH=11 (Check Keyboard Buffer)

This function merely reports the status of the keyboard buffer, i.e., whether or not it has a character waiting. Upon return, if AL=FF, a character is waiting in the buffer. If AL=0, no character is waiting. This routine also checks for the Break key.

If you are planning to use function 1, 7, or 8 to retrieve a character from the keyboard, you may want to use this function first to check if one is ready; otherwise, the program will halt all operations and wait for character input.

AH=12 (Clear Keyboard Buffer—Invoke an Input Function)

This function clears the keyboard buffer before reading new input, which is useful in data entry programs where data is entered at considerable speed and an overflow of input may frequently occur, thus plugging up the keyboard buffer. You can use this function to clear the buffer of the overflow characters each time you move to another record or field.

Once the buffer is cleared, this function also invokes one of the other keyboard input functions (1, 6, 7, or 8), depending on the value in the AL register. From the discussion of input functions, remember that all but one of these functions (6) force the program to wait for input. Once again, if you do not want the program to cease all operations and wait for input, use function 6.

Procedure ClearKBDBuffer uses DOS function 12H to clear the keyboard buffer. You may want to include it in your library of subroutines for Turbo Pascal or use it as a separate Include file to be called from any program during compilation.

The type definition for RegSet is as follows:

```
Type
  RegSet = record
             case Integer of
               1: (AX, BX, CX, DX, BP, SI, DI, DS, ES, Flags: Integer);
               2: (AH, AL, BH, BL, CH, CL, DH, DL           : Byte    );
           end;

     Procedure ClearKBDBuffer;
     var
       Regs : RegSet;        { the register set }

     begin
        Regs.AH := $0C;     { requesting function #12          }
        Regs.AL := $06;     { followed by #6 for keyboard input }
        Regs.DL := $FF;
        MsDos(Regs);         { DOS function call                }
     end;
```

CHAPTER 15

ERROR HANDLING IN DOS

A DOS critical error occurs when the drive door is accidentally left open and when no floppy, an unformatted floppy, or a write-protected floppy (and you are attempting to write to the disk) is inserted in the drive. An error also occurs when the printer is out of paper, jammed, or disconnected.

A Ctrl-Break or Ctrl-C key combination is often used to "break" out of or terminate the current process (a program or an operation).

Implementing a proper DOS critical error service routine as well as a Ctrl-Break key service routine is often of low priority for many software developers. You may recall numerous applications in which you were often prompted with the notorious "Abort, Retry, Ignore" message when the drive door was left open accidentally or when there was no floppy in the drive. (For example, try accessing a drive with the door open in the Turbo Pascal Editor.)

To make things worse, this "Abort, Retry, Ignore" message generally overwrites some part of the screen created by the application. Since the application has no built-in scheme for handling this situation, it also does not anticipate it. Until the application rewrites the screen, the message becomes an annoying fixture on the screen, often as a side effect causing the screen to scroll up.

Also, giving an inexperienced user the option of aborting, retrying, or ignoring a critical error can, in many cases, mean devastating results for the application, especially if the prompt is misunderstood.

Similarly, many applications do not have any special Ctrl-Break traps. They allow frustrated users to exit the application using the Ctrl-Break keys. As you well know, Ctrl-Break is DOS's way of providing an "abnormal" exit from the current application. This type of exit has many implications including potential loss of data since data files are not closed properly when an application terminates abnormally.

Furthermore, if the application is part of a complex job stream, then the implications also ride on to the next process that is to be executed since, upon terminating a program, DOS transfers control to the next statement in the batch stream, and that process may very likely depend on the output from the previous one.

As you will see in this chapter, these problems have relatively simple solutions. DOS provides a way for you to write your own custom routines to handle the Ctrl-Break keys as well as critical errors.

In the simplest case, you have the option to exit or resume the program when a Ctrl-Break is detected and display more meaningful error messages and prompts in a pop-up window or the predefined status line when critical errors occur, thereby preserving the application screen.

Implementing a more sophisticated user-written Ctrl-Break interrupt service routine may involve using the Ctrl-Break keys to initiate or terminate specific functions in an application rather than to exit from the application.

This chapter discusses creating Ctrl-break and critical error handling routines in Turbo Pascal using Inline machine code. The two topics are related only to the extent that the techniques involved in handling both are very similar. The BIOS and DOS interrupts and function calls involved in the processes are also reviewed.

HANDLING INTERRUPTS

Interrupts were introduced in Chapter 3. A general discussion of BIOS and DOS interrupts and DOS function calls associated with Interrupt type 21H is provided in Chapter 9. Before proceeding with this chapter, you may want to review backgrounds of these interrupts in the appropriate chapters.

To briefly review the interrupt process, remember that an interrupt is generated via a specific signal, such as when you press the Control and Break keys simultaneously. DOS actually detects the Ctrl-Break signal during standard I/O to the display monitor, printer, or serial communications device.

As a result of the interrupt signal, control is transferred to the routine that processes that interrupt. In the case of the Ctrl-Break key detection, DOS interrupt 23H is invoked. The vector for this interrupt is located in low memory at segment address 0. For current DOS and BIOS versions, you can calculate the offset by multiplying the number of the interrupt "type" by 4 (23H x 4 = 8CH).

When DOS detects the Ctrl-Break flag set during a function request for standard I/O, it transfers control to the routine at the address provided by the Intr 23H vector. Normally, this transfer results in abnormal termination of the program, with the control transferred to the command interpreter.

To replace the interrupt service routine associated with Intr 23H with your own routine, you have to replace its vector with the starting address of your routine. DOS function 35H (get vector) is used to access the current value of the interrupt vector. Similarly, DOS function 25H (set vector) sets the new value for the user-written interrupt service.

For two reasons, it is recommended that you preserve the original vector (address of the original routine).

First, you may want to simply trap and monitor the interrupt so that you have the option of resuming the current task or transferring control to another (resident) task. For example, RAM-resident programs like SideKick take over the keyboard interrupt and monitor every key pressed. In this case, control is transferred to the resident application (SideKick) only when it detects the hot key (Ctrl-Alt).

Second, you also want to restore the original vector when you are done with your task; however, in the case of the Ctrl-Break action, DOS automatically restores the original vector when the program terminates. In this case, maintaining a user-written Ctrl-Break interrupt service routine for more than one application is yet another challenge.

Interrupt Service Routines (ISR) in Turbo Pascal

When writing your own **ISR**'s (interrupt service routines), you must preserve all registers that you intend to use in the ISR. This guarantees that when control is returned from the ISR, the task invoking the interrupt can resume normal execution.

Furthermore, Borland strongly recommends not only saving registers that you intend to use but saving all of the registers before transferring control to the ISR. Following this transfer, register values are restored prior to exiting the ISR, as shown here.

Somewhere in the program:

```
{ ISR Entry }
Inline($13            { push DS }
       /$50           { push AX }
       /$53           { push BX }
       /$51           { push CX }
       /$52           { push DX }
       /$56           { push SI }
       /$57           { push DI }
       /$06);         { push ES }

Inline($2E
       /$A1
       /DSSAVE        { mov AX,CS:[DSSAVE] }
       /$8E/$D8);     { mov DS,AX }

{ pascal source code }

{ ISR Return }
Inline($07            { pop ES }
       /$5F           { pop DI }
       /$5E           { pop SI }
       /$5A           { pop DX }
       /$59           { pop CX }
       /$5B           { pop BX }
       /$58           { pop AX }
       /$1F           { pop DS }
       /$8B/$ED       { mov SP,BP }
       /$5D           { pop BP }
       /$CF);         { iret     }
```

In addition to saving registers, as indicated above, you may need to enable interrupts (STI), depending on the particular interrupt you are processing.

The second Inline statement moves the starting address of Turbo's data segment into the DS register. Following this instruction, you can access variables defined in your Turbo Pascal program within the ISR.

The reason for restoring DS should be obvious. When an ISR is invoked, control can be within the application, DOS, or some other coresident utility; therefore, the ISR does not know where the current DS is pointing. To circumvent this problem, and if you want access to variables defined in the main program, restore Turbo's data segment register after all registers have been saved in the ISR.

Note that you cannot (and must not attempt to) access local variables defined in other subroutines in your ISR.

Borland also recommends a technique for restoring the data register, which involves defining a typed constant (an initialized data structure in the code segment) in which the value of DS is saved at the start of the program. The following Turbo Pascal statement performs the function:

```
const
   DSSAVE : integer = 0; { defining a typed constant }

{ at the start of the main program code }
begin
  DSSAVE := DSeg            { saving the value in DS    }
```

DSeg is Turbo's built-in integer function that returns the current contents of the DS register.

Another technique, as suggested by Paul Dunphy in "IBM PC Interrupt Service Routines" in *Byte* (Fall, 1985), involves defining an absolute variable at the bottom of the code segment (somewhere in words 5 through 15) as follows:

```
var
  DSSAVE : integer absolute CSEG:$0006;

begin
  DSSAVE := DSeg;
```

And in the ISR, the second Inline statement would be as follows:

```
Inline($8C/$C8          { mov AX,CS     }
      /$8E/$D8          { mov DS,AX     }
      /$A1/DSSAVE       { mov AX,DSSAVE }
      /$8E/$D8);        { mov DS,AX     }
```

In this example, the CS register is copied into the DS so that you can access the absolute variable DSSAVE. Then, the contents of the absolute variable are moved into the DS register. This technique is based on the premise that the top of the code segment of a Turbo Pascal program (where the absolute variable is declared) does not contain any executable code or any other data item of value since you overwrite it with the variable declaration.

In some cases, you may also need to tell the **PIC** (the 8259 Programmable Interrupt Controller) that you are through processing the interrupt service, which is done by sending an **EOI** (End Of Interrupt) command to the PIC—a hex 20 to the port 20H. The following Turbo Pascal statement accomplishes this task:

```
const
    EOI = $20;

port[$20] := EOI;
```

Turbo's **port** array provides Read/Write access to the I/O ports of the PC's 8088 processor. In the above statement, the value 20H is also outputted to port number 20H.

You can do the same in an Inline statement:

```
Inline($B0/$20              { mov al,20H }
      /$E6/$20);            { out 20,al  }
```

When processing several interrupts, the PIC waits until one is processed before it transfers control to the ISR of the next in line. An example of this type of interrupt is BIOS interrupt 1BH (Ctrl-Break check) discussed later in this chapter.

REVIEWING BIOS AND DOS INTERRUPTS

The following BIOS and DOS interrupts and DOS functions are discussed in relation to interrupt handling techniques in this chapter:

- DOS Interrupt 23H—Ctrl-Break Address
- BIOS Interrupt 1BH—Keyboard Break Address
- DOS Function 33H—Ctrl-Break Check
- DOS Function 35H—Get vector
- DOS Function 25H—Set vector

DOS Interrupt 23H—Control-Break Address

Interrupt 23H (decimal 35) is generated when DOS detects the Ctrl-Break or Ctrl-C action at the keyboard.

Both Ctrl-Break and Ctrl-C actions have the same effect in a program, i.e., to exit abnormally. The control is returned to the DOS command interpreter. Since the key action is used to break out of programs, the combination is often referred to for convenience as a "break key."

Normally, the break key is only detected when a program engages in standard DOS input from the keyboard, output to the display or printer, and communications with the asynchronous communications adapter (the serial RS 232C port).

However, when you specify BREAK=ON at the DOS prompt or BREAK=ON in the CONFIG.SYS file or through DOS function 33H (Ctrl-Break check/set), DOS checks for the break key action on most I/O operations including disk I/O, with the exception of direct console I/O (function 6H) and direct console input without echo (function 7H).

As a side effect, having DOS check for the break key action tends to slow down the already slow I/O operations. This DOS check is analogous to the Ctrl-Break key checking in Turbo Pascal, which can be turned off in a program via the **C Compiler Directive**. This directive is "ON" by default, and you can specify {C-} at the top of the program to turn it off, i.e., exclude break key checking that will interrupt a program during Read/ReadLn operations if a break key is detected.

In relation to Intr 23H, DOS allows you to replace the routine that Intr 23H invokes by default with your own break key service routine. In your program, you may want to completely ignore the break key and continue with program execution, use it selectively for specific functions, or use it to exit from the program and give the user the option. In any case, if you write your own break key service routine, you are free to process the break key as you want.

A discussion of custom break key service routines to replace Intr 23H routines is presented later in this chapter.

BIOS Interrupt 1BH—Keyboard Break Address

In addition to DOS monitoring the break key action, the PC's BIOS also monitors it through BIOS interrupt 1BH. As with DOS Intr 23H, BIOS Intr 1BH points to an interrupt service routine that takes control whenever the break key is detected. Normally, this routine simply sets a flag and returns control with an IRET without any action; however, as always, you can replace this routine with a custom interrupt service routine of your own to process the break key action.

There are two major differences between Intr 1BH and 23H. First, a user-written break key service routine that replaces 23H is only active during execution of the program that sets it. Upon termination of that program, DOS resets this service routine to the original routine; therefore, you cannot make this interrupt service routine resident for more than one program at a time. In contrast, the BIOS Intr 1BH service routine is active for as long as it is needed until the PC is rebooted or turned off.

Second, the mechanism by which each interrupt takes charge is different. Intr 1BH is generated as a result of a hardware interrupt, which implies that it takes control every time a Ctrl-Break key action is detected. Barring any interrupt disable requests prior to Ctrl-Break, this process is immediate.

In contrast, DOS only checks (or acts upon) the break key when an I/O function is requested. If the program is in a processing loop and not performing any I/O, then Ctrl-Break will produce no action from DOS until the request for I/O is made through one of the function calls that does not ignore Ctrl-Break.

Note that the two interrupts require different service routines. Most programmers are content to replace the service routine for DOS's Intr 23H with a custom routine and enable Ctrl-Break checking using function 33H (Ctrl-Break check), which increases DOS's responsiveness to the break keys and allows the custom routine to process break keys more efficiently.

Writing an interrupt service routine for 1BH would be quite efficient for Ctrl-Break checking; however, it is also very difficult, since this interrupt is hardware-generated and outside of DOS. When such an interrupt occurs, it is not clear whether the current application or DOS has the control. If you wish to write a service routine for this interrupt, you may want to remember a few pointers:

- Save all the registers before entering the interrupt service routine.
- Save the SS and SP registers, and use a new stack if needed.
- Enable interrupts and reset all I/O devices in the event the interrupt was generated at a time when an operation was being performed.
- Send one or more End-Of-Interrupt (EOI) commands to the Programmable Interrupt Controller (PIC).
- Since Intr 1BH is not part of DOS, it is not restored by DOS when a program terminates; therefore, the program is responsible for restoring its original routine prior to termination.

DOS Function 33H—Ctrl-Break Check

DOS function 33H is a dual-purpose function and is used for checking as well as setting the value of DOS's Ctrl-Break checking flag.

If AL is 0 upon entry to the function, then the function returns the current state of the Ctrl-Break checking flag. On return, the DL register contains the status of Ctrl-Break checking (the value in the flag). If the value is 0, Ctrl-Break checking is off; if the value is 1, the checking is on.

To set Ctrl-Break checking, the AL register must be 1 or 2 upon entry to the function routine. If the register is 1, then the value in DL is moved to the Ctrl-Break checking flag. If it is 2, the value in DL is exchanged with the Ctrl-Break flag.

By setting the Ctrl-Break checking flag, DOS can check for Ctrl-Break keys during most of the I/O operations, as discussed earlier. This function, therefore, provides "extended" Ctrl-Break checking.

Similarly, by turning off "extended" Ctrl-Break checking using this function, you can prevent certain I/O operations from being interrupted. Limitations associated with this function were noted earlier.

Following is a summary of the register values for the two options associated with Function 33H.

Get status of Ctrl-Break checking flag:

On entry

```
AL = 0              get flag
```

On return

```
DL = 0              if Ctrl-Break checking is off
DL = 1              if Ctrl-Break checking is on
```

Set Ctrl-Break checking:

On entry

```
AL = 1          set flag
AL = 2          exchange flag with DL

DL = 0          set checking off
DL = 1          set checking on
```

DOS Function 35H—Get Vector

DOS Function 35H returns the address (vector) of the interrupt service routine whose number is specified in the AL register upon entry. The address of the interrupt type is returned in the register pair ES:BX.

This function is mostly useful for obtaining the current address of a specific interrupt service routine when you want to preserve it for later restoration.

On entry

```
AL = interrupt number
```

On return

```
ES = segment address (CS of interrupt service routine)
BX = offset address (IP of interrupt service routine)
```

If you are familiar with interrupt vectors and the vector table, you will see that there is a quick and dirty method of obtaining an interrupt vector by peeking at the vector table; however, that method is not recommended since, in the long run, using such techniques compromises the compatibility factor with newer versions of DOS.

Program 15.1 demonstrates the use of this function to get interrupt vectors. It displays the first 20 vectors. You can further modify it to display addresses of select ISRs. For convenience, the program outputs the address in segment:offset format in hex.

Program 15.1

```
(* ---------------------------------------------------------------*)
(* Program 15-1                                         4/10/87 *)
(* Author: Sanjiva Nath                               Version 1  *)
(*                                                               *)
(* Description: Getting the interrupt vector using DOS's         *)
(*              Function 35H.                                    *)
(*                                                               *)
(* -------------------------------------------------------------- *)

Program IntVector;

Type
    RegSet = record
               case Integer of
                 1: (AX, BX, CX, DX, BP, SI, DI, DS, ES, Flags: Integer);
                 2: (AL, AH, BL, BH, CL, CH, DL, DH          : Byte    );
               end;
   vector = record
             Seg   : integer;     { segment address }
             Ofs   : integer;     { offset address  }
            end;

   HexStr = string[4];
   Str4   = string[4];
   HexVal = string[4];

var
   IntrVec    : vector;
   IntrType   : integer;
   Segment, Offset : HexVal;

const
   GetIntrVec : byte = $35;

Function HexConvert(ArgIn : Byte): HexStr;
{ converts a byte into the hexadecimal format,
  returns a string representing the hex value  }
const
   HexTabl : array[0..15] of Char = '0123456789ABCDEF';
var
   HiByte, LoByte: Char;
begin
   HiByte := HexTabl[ArgIn shr 4];      { convert the high bits }
   LoByte := HexTabl[ArgIn AND 15];     { convert the low bits  }
   HexConvert := HiByte + LoByte;       { concatenate strings   }
end;


Procedure ConvertHex(Arg:integer; var HexArg:Str4);
```

continued...

...from previous page

```
{ convert integer into hex representation using HexConvert }
begin
  HexArg := HexConvert(Hi(Arg)) + HexConvert(Lo(Arg));
end;

Procedure GetIntVector(IntrNo:Byte;var IntVec:vector);
var
  Regs : RegSet;
begin
   Regs.AH := GetIntrVec;      { Ah always contains the function no }
   Regs.AL := IntrNo;          { interrupt type in AL               }
   Intr($21,Regs);             { Requesting DOS's Intr 21H          }

   IntVec.Seg := Regs.ES;      { segment address returned in ES     }
   IntVec.Ofs := Regs.BX;      { offset address returned in BX      }
end; { procedure GetIntVector }


{ main program begins here }

begin
   Write('Interrupt Type                ');
   WriteLn('Service Routine Address');
   For IntrType := 0 to 20  do
      begin
        GetIntVector(IntrType,IntrVec);
        ConvertHex(IntrVec.Seg,Segment);
        ConvertHex(IntrVec.Ofs,Offset);
        Write('      ',IntrType:2,'
        WriteLn(Segment,':',Offset);
      end;
end.
```

DOS Function 25H—Set Vector

DOS Function 25H sets the new address (vector) of the interrupt service routine whose number is specified in the AL register upon entry. The address of the interrupt service routine is specified in the register pair DS:DX.

This function is used for replacing the interrupt service routine with a user-written routine.

On entry

```
AL = interrupt number
DS = segment address (CS of interrupt service routine)
DX = offset address (IP of interrupt service routine)
```

CHECKING CONTROL-BREAKS

If writing custom interrupt service routines is a hassle, there are a few crude measures you can take to process the break keys. These measures, as suggested in the now defunct *MS DOS Technical Reference Encyclopedia*, are as follows:

- Use DOS function 6H (direct console I/O) and 7H (input without echo) to check or read keyboard (standard input device) input, and use 6H to display output to the monitor (standard output device).

  This is recommended simply because these functions do not check for the Ctrl-Break keys. However, notice the limitations since I/O is limited to two functions.

- Perform output to the monitor by directly writing to the video memory.

  DOS can only check for Ctrl-Break action during an I/O via one of the function calls. If a program does not invoke any of DOS's I/O services, there is little or no opportunity to trap the break keys. Most commercial applications write directly to video memory to speed up screen I/O.

- Disable Control-Break checking through service 33H of Interrupt 21H.

  A primary limitation here is that this service will not disable break key checking during standard I/O, output to the printer, or communications with the asynchronous adapter.

As noted, these methods are either partially effective or limiting. The recommended method is by far the custom interrupt service routine in which you can specify the action to be taken when a break key is detected.

HANDLING CRITICAL ERRORS

As mentioned earlier in this chapter, a critical error occurs when DOS attempts to access a file on a drive and finds either no floppy in the drive, the drive door open, an unformatted disk, or corrupted data in the file.

Similarly, a critical error occurs when DOS makes an attempt to output data to a printer, and the printer does not respond because it is jammed, out of paper or ribbon, or off-line.

In any case, when DOS encounters a critical error, interrupt type 24H is generated. As a consequence of Int 24H, you are prompted with the familiar "Abort, Retry, Ignore?" message. Abort terminates the current task via interrupt 23H. Retry forces DOS to retry the operation. Ignore forces DOS to ignore the error (i.e., pretends that it succeeded in performing the I/O operation).

This prompt also expects a single character (A, I, or R) of input from the user. An "Abort" here could mean termination of the current task, loss of data in memory, loss of data on disk in files that were not closed properly, and so on. In other words, accidentally aborting an application following this prompt could be disastrous. An "Ignore" could force bad data to be loaded into memory, causing the system to halt.

The answer is to write your own ISR to handle critical errors. You can prompt the user with more meaningful messages and at least not give the option to terminate the current task.

The guidelines for writing custom ISR's were discussed earlier in this chapter. In this section, a brief discussion is presented of processing and recovering from DOS critical errors.

DOS Critical Errors

When DOS encounters a critical error, it executes INT 24H, transferring control to the service routine for that interrupt. The error is indicated in the AH register; therefore, after preserving the registers, the ISR should first check the AH register to determine the type of error.

Based on the value returned in the AH register, DOS classifies critical errors as one of two types:

- If bit 7 of the AH register is set to 0, the error occurred during a disk I/O operation
- If bit 7 of the AH register is set to 1, the error occurred elsewhere

Furthermore, for disk-related errors, the AL register contains the drive number, starting with 0 for A, 1 for B, and so on. Also, bit 0 of the AH register indicates the type of operation, i.e., read (bit 0 = 0) or write (bit 0 = 1) requested when the error occurred. Finally, bits 1 and 2 indicate the specific area where the error occurred, as shown here:

Bits →	2 1	
	0 0	(DOS system files)
	0 1	(FAT)
	1 0	(directory)
	1 1	(user files)

The BP:SI register pair points to a Device Header Control Block, which contains further information on the error.

The DL register contains the error code. Table 15.1 presents the error codes in the DH register and their corresponding error conditions as presented in the *DOS Technical Reference Manual.*

Table 15.1 Critical Error Code

CODE	ERROR CONDITION
0	Write-protected disk
1	Unknown unit
2	Drive door open
3	Unknown command
4	Checksum error on read
5	Bad request structure length
6	Seek error
7	Unknown media type
8	Sector not found
9	Printer out of paper
A	Write fault
B	Read Fault
C	General device failure

On return from the interrupt service routine, DOS takes back the response in the AL register, requesting to abort (AL=2), ignore the error (AL=0), retry (AL=1), or fail the system call that is in progress (AL=3).

APPENDICES

APPENDIX A: THE ASCII TABLE

This list contains the standard 128-item ASCII Code Set, numbered in decimal and binary. The binary numbers show only seven bits of the typical eight-bit bytes used in transfers. Not listed are the non-standard "high codes" (128-255), which are part of IBM's Extended ASCII set and include special graphics characters, scientific symbols, and foreign language symbols.

Except for the <ESC> key (27), most personal computer keyboards do not have special keys for codes 0 through 31; however, the list shows Ctrl, Shift, and character key combinations that can command those codes.

DEC	BINARY	ASCII	KEY COMBINATION
0	(0000000)	NUL	CTRL-SHFT-P
1	(0000001)	SOH	CTRL-A
2	(0000010)	STX	CTRL-B
3	(0000011)	ETX	CTRL-C
4	(0000100)	EOT	CTRL-D
5	(0000101)	ENQ	CTRL-E
6	(0000110)	ACK	CTRL-F
7	(0000111)	BEL	CTRL-G
8	(0001000)	BS	CTRL-H
9	(0001001)	HT	CTRL-I
10	(0001010)	LF	CTRL-J
11	(0001011)	VT	CTRL-K
12	(0001100)	FF	CTRL-L
13	(0001101)	CR	CTRL-M
14	(0001110)	SO	CTRL-N
15	(0001111)	SI	CTRL-O
16	(0010000)	DLE	CTRL-P
17	(0010001)	DC1	CTRL-Q
18	(0010010)	DC2	CTRL-R
19	(0010011)	DC3	CTRL-S
20	(0010100)	DC4	CTRL-T
21	(0010101)	NAK	CTRL-U
22	(0010110)	SYN	CTRL-V
23	(0010111)	ETB	CTRL-W
24	(0011000)	CAN	CTRL-X

continued...

DEC	BINARY	ASCII	KEY COMBINATION
25	(0011001)	EM	CTRL-Y
26	(0011010)	SUB	CTRL-Z
27	(0011011)	ESC	CTRL-SHFT-K
28	(0011100)	FS	CTRL-SHFT-L
29	(0011101)	GS	CTRL-SHFT-M
30	(0011110)	RS	CTRL-SHFT-N
31	(0011111)	US	CTRL-SHFT-O
32	(0100000)	SP	SPACEBAR
33	(0100001)	! (Exclamation Point)	
34	(0100010)	" (Quotation Mark)	
35	(0100011)	# (Pound Sign)	
36	(0100100)	$ (Dollar Sign)	
37	(0100101)	% (Percentage Sign)	
38	(0100110)	& (Ampersand)	
39	(0100111)	' (Apostrophe or Single Quote)	
40	(0101000)	((Left Parenthesis)	
41	(0101001)	) (Right Parenthesis)	
42	(0101010)	* (Asterisk)	
43	(0101011)	+ (Plus Sign)	
44	(0101100)	, (Comma)	
45	(0101101)	- (Hyphen)	
46	(0101110)	. (Period)	
47	(0101111)	/ (Slash)	
48	(0110000)	0	
49	(0110001)	1	
50	(0110010)	2	
51	(0110011)	3	
52	(0110100)	4	
53	(0110101)	5	
54	(0110110)	6	
55	(0110111)	7	
56	(0111000)	8	
57	(0111001)	9	
58	(0111010)	: (Colon)	
59	(0111011)	; (Semicolon)	
60	(0111100)	< (Less Than)	
61	(0111101)	= (Equals)	
62	(0111110)	> (Greater Than)	
63	(0111111)	? (Question Mark)	
64	(1000000)	@ (At Sign)	
65	(1000001)	A	

continued...

DEC	BINARY	ASCII
66	(1000010)	B
67	(1000011)	C
68	(1000100)	D
69	(1000101)	E
70	(1000110)	F
71	(1000111)	G
72	(1001000)	H
73	(1001001)	I
74	(1001010)	J
75	(1001011)	K
76	(1001100)	L
77	(1001101)	M
78	(1001110)	N
79	(1001111)	O
80	(1010000)	P
81	(1010001)	Q
82	(1010010)	R
83	(1010011)	S
84	(1010100)	T
85	(1010101)	U
86	(1010110)	V
87	(1010111)	W
88	(1011000)	X
89	(1011001)	Y
90	(1011010)	Z
91	(1011011)	[(Left Bracket)
92	(1011100)	\ (Reverse Slant)
93	(1011101)	] (Right Bracket)
94	(1011110)	^ (Caret)
95	(1011111)	_ (Underline)
96	(1100000)	` (Opening Single Quote)
97	(1100001)	a
98	(1100010)	b
99	(1100011)	c
100	(1100100)	d
101	(1100101)	e
102	(1100110)	f
103	(1100111)	g
104	(1101000)	h
105	(1101001)	i
106	(1101010)	j

continued...

DEC	BINARY	ASCII
107	(1101011)	k
108	(1101100)	l
109	(1101101)	m
110	(1101110)	n
111	(1101111)	o
112	(1110000)	p
113	(1110001)	q
114	(1110010)	r
115	(1110011)	s
116	(1110100)	t
117	(1110101)	u
118	(1110110)	v
119	(1110111)	w
120	(1111000)	x
121	(1111001)	y
122	(1111010)	z
123	(1111011)	{ (Left Brace)
124	(1111100)	| (Vertical Line)
125	(1111101)	} (Right Brace)
126	(1111110)	~ (Tilde Mark)
127	(1111111)	DEL (Delete or Rub out)

APPENDIX B: THE 8088 INSTRUCTION SET

Mnemonic	Description
Data Transfer	
MOV	Move
PUSH	Push Word onto Stack
POP	Pop Word Off Stack to Destination
XCHG	Exchange Two Operands
IN	Input Byte or Word
OUT	Output Byte or Word
XLAT	Translate
LEA	Load Effective Address
LDS	Load Pointer Using DS
LES	Load Pointer Using ES
LAHF	Load AH from Flags
SAHF	Store AH into Flags
PUSHF	Push Flags onto Stack
POPF	Pop Flags Off Stack
Arithmetic Instructions	
ADD	Add (without Carry)
SBB	Subtract with Borrow
DEC	Decrement Destination by One
NEG	Negate
CMP	Compare Destination to Source
ADC	Add with Carry
INC	Increment Destination by One
AAA	ASCII Adjust for Addition
DAA	Decimal Adjust for Addition
SUB	Subtract (Without Borrow)
AAS	ASCII Adjust for Subtraction
DAS	Decimal Adjust for Subtraction
MUL	Multiply (Unsigned)
IMUL	Integer Multiply (Signed)
AAM	ASCII Adjust for Multiplication
DIV	Divide (Unsigned)
IDIV	Integer Divide (Signed)
AAD	ASCII Adjust for Division
CBW	Convert Byte to Word
CWD	Convert Word to Double Word
Logical Instructions	
NOT	Logical NOT
SHL/SAL	Shift Arithmetic Left/Logical Left

continued...

Mnemonic	Description
SHR	Shift Logical Right
SAR	Shift Arithmetic Right
ROL	Rotate Left
ROR	Rotate Right
RCL	Rotate Left through Carry
RCR	Rotate Right through Carry
AND	Logical AND
TEST	Test (Logical AND)
OR	Logical OR
XOR	Logical eXclusive OR

String Instructions

REP	Repeat String Operation
MOVS	Move Byte or Word String
CMPS	Compare Byte or Word Strings
SCAS	Scan Byte or Word String
LODS	Load Byte or Word String
STOS	Store Byte or Word String

Control Transfer Instructions

CALL	Procedure Call
JMP	Jump Unconditionally
RET	Procedure Return
JE/JZ	Jump If Equal/If Zero
JL/JNGE	Jump If Less/If Not Greater Nor Equal
JLE/JNG	Jump If Less Or Equal/If Not Greater
JB/JNAE	Jump If Below/If Not ABOVE nor Equal/If Carry
JBE/JNA	Jump If Below or Equal/If Not Above
JP/JPE	Jump On Parity/If Parity Even
JO	Jump On Overflow
JS	Jump On Sign
JNE/JNZ	Jump If Not Equal/If Not Zero
JNL/JGE	Jump If Less Or Equal/If Not Greater
JNLE/JG	Jump If Greater/If Not Less nor Equal
JNB/JAE	Jump If Above or Equal/If Not Below/If No Car
JNBE/JA	Jump If Above/If Not Below nor Equal
JNP/JPO	Jump If No Parity/If Parity Odd
JNS	Jump If No Sign (If Positive)
LOOP	Loop Until Count Complete
LOOPZ/LOOPE	Loop While Equal/While Zero
LOOPNZ/LOOPNE	Loop While Not Equal/While Not Zero
JCXZ	Jump If CX Is Zero

continued...

Mnemonic	Description
Processor Control Instructions	
INT	Interrupt
INTO	Interrupt If Overflow
IRET	Interrupt Return
CLC	Clear Carry Flag
CMC	Complement Carry Flag
CLD	Clear Direction Flag
CLI	Clear Interrupt Flag
HLT	Halt the Processor
LOCK	Lock the Bus
STC	Set Carry Flag
NOP	No Operation
STD	Set Direction Flag
STI	Set Interrupt Enable Flag
WAIT	Wait
ESC	Escape

APPENDIX C: THE INSTRUCTION SET SUMMARY

Instruction	Byte 1	Byte 2	Byte 3	Byte 4
Data Transfer Instructions				
MOV				
Reg/Mem To/From Reg	100010dw	mod reg r/m		
Immed To Reg/Mem	1100011w	mod 000 r/m	data-low	data-high
Immed To Reg	1011wreg	data	data if w 1	
Mem to Accumulator	1010000w	addr-low	addr-high	
Accumulator to Mem	1010001w	addr-low	addr-high	
Reg/Mem to Segment Reg	10001110	mod 0 reg r/m		
Segment Reg to Reg/Mem	10001100	mod 0 reg r/m		
PUSH				
Reg/Mem	11111111	mod 110 r/m		
Reg	01010 reg			
Segment Reg	000 reg 110			
POP				
Reg/Mem	10001111	mod 000 r/m		
Reg	01011 reg			
Segment Reg	000 reg 111			
XCHG				
Reg/Mem With Reg	1000011w	mod reg r/m		
Reg with Accumulator	10010 reg			
IN				
Fixed port	1110010w	port		
Variable port	1110110w			
OUT				
Fixed port	1110011w	port		
Variable port	1110110w			
XLAT	11010111			
LEA	10001101	mod reg r/m		
LDS	11000101	mod reg r/m		
LES	11000100	mod reg r/m		
LAHF	10011111			
SAHF	10011110			
PUSHF	10011100			
POPF	10011101			
Arithmetic Instructions				
ADD				
Reg Mem with Reg to Either	000000dw	mod reg r/m		
Immediate to Reg Mem	100000sw	mod 000 r/m	data	data if s:w=01
Immediate to Accum	0000010w	data	data if w = 1	
ADC				
Reg/Mem with Reg to either	000100dw	mod reg r/m		
Immediate to Reg/Mem	100000sw	mod 010 r/m	data	data if s:w=1
Immediate to Accum	0001010w	data	data if w=1	
INC				
Reg/Mem	1111111w	mod 000 r/m		
Reg	01000 reg			
AAA	00110111			
DAA	00100111			

continued...

Instruction	Byte 1	Byte 2	Byte 3	Byte 4
SUB				
Reg/Mem & Reg to either	000110dw	mod reg r/m		
Immediate from Reg /Mem	100000sw	mod 101 r/m	data	data if s:w=01
Immediate from Accum	0010110w	data	data if w=01	
SBB				
Reg/Mem & Reg to either	000110dw	mod reg r/m		
Immediate from Reg/ Mem	100000sw	mod 011 r/m	data if s:w=01	
Immediate from Accum	0001110w	data	data if w = 1	
DEC				
Reg/Mem	1111111w	mod 001 r/m		
Reg	01001 reg			
NEG	1111011w	mod 011 r/m		
CMP				
Reg/Mem & Reg	001110dw	mod reg r/m		
Immediate with Reg/ Mem	100000sw	mod 111 r/m	data	data if s:w=01
Immediate with Accum	0011110w	data	data if w 1	
AAS	00111111			
DAS	00101111			
MUL	1111011w	mod 100 r/m		
IMUL	1111011w	mod 101 r/m		
AAM	11010100	00001010		
DIV	1111011w	mod 110 r/m		
IDIV	1111011w	mod 111 r/m		
AAD	11010101	00001010		
CBW	10011000			
CWD	10011001			

Logic Instructions

Instruction	Byte 1	Byte 2	Byte 3	Byte 4
NOT	1111011w	mod 010 r/m		
SHL/SAL	110100vw	mod 100 r/m		
SHR	110100vw	mod 101 r/m		
SAR	110100vw	mod 111 r/m		
ROL	110100vw	mod 000 r/m		
ROR	110100vw	mod 001 r/m		
RCL	110100vw	mod 010 r/m		
RCR	110100vw	mod 011 r/m		
AND				
REG/MEM & REG to either	001000dw	mod reg r/m		
Immediate to Reg/Mem	1000000w	mod 100 r/m	data	data if w=1
Immediate to Accum	0010010w	data	data if w=1	
TEST				
Reg/Mem & Reg	1000010w	mod reg r/m		
Immediate data & Reg/ Mem	1111011w	mod 000 r/m	data	data if w=1
Immediate data & Accum	1010100w	data	data if w=1	
OR				
Reg/Mem & Reg	000010dw	mod reg r/m		
Immediate to Reg/Mem	1000000w	mod 001 r/m	data	data if w=1

continued...

Instruction	Byte 1	Byte 2	Byte 3	Byte 4
Immediate to Accum	0000110w	data	data if w=1	
XOR				
Reg/Mem & Reg to either	001100dw	mod reg r/m		
Immediate to Reg/Mem	1000000w	mod 110 r/m	data	data if w=1
Immediate to Accum	0011010w	data	data if w=1	

String Manipulation Instructions

REP	1111001z			
MOVS	1010010w			
CMPS	1010011w			
SCAS	1010111w			
LODS	1010110w			
STDS	1010101w			

Control Transfer Instructions

CALL				
Direct within Seg	11101000	disp-low	disp-high	
Indirect within Seg	11111111	mod 010 r/m		
Direct intersegment	10011010	offset-low seg-low	offset-high seg-high	
Indirect intersegment	11111111	mod 011 r/m		
JMP				
Direct within Seg	11101001	disp-low	disp-high	
Direct within Seg-short	11101011	disp		
Indirect within Seg	11111111	mod 100 r/m		
Direct intersegment	11101010	offset-low seg-low	offset-high seg-high	
Indirect intersegment	11111111	mod 101r/m		
RET				
Within Segment	11000011			
Within seg adding immed to SP	11000010	data-low	data-high	
Intersegment	11001011			
Intersegment adding immediate to SP	11001010	data-low	data-high	
JE/JZ	01110100	disp		
JL/JNGE	01111100	disp		
JLE/JNG	01111110	disp		
JB/JNAE	01110010	disp		
JBE/JNA	01110110	disp		
JP/JPE	01111010	disp		
JO	01110000	disp		
JS	01111000	disp		
JNE/JNZ	01110101	disp		
JNL/JGE	01111101	disp		
JNLE/JG	01111111	disp		
JNB/JAE	01110011	disp		
JNBE/JA	01110111	disp		
JNP/JPO	01111011	disp		
JNO	01110001	disp		
JNS	01111001	disp		
LOOP	11100010	disp		
LOOPZ/LOOPE	11100001	disp		
LOOPNZ/LOOPNE	11100000	disp		
JCXZ	11100011	disp		

continued...

Instruction	Byte 1	Byte 2	Byte 3	Byte 4
INT				
Type specified	11001101	type		
Type 3	11001100			
INTO	11001110			
IRET	11001111			

Processor Control Instructions

CLC	11111000			
CMC	11110101			
STC	11111001			
CLD	11111100			
STD	11111101			
CLI	11111010			
STI	11111011			
HLT	11110100			
WAIT	10011011			
ESC	11011xxx	mod xxx r/m		
LOCK	11110000			

Notes:

w = 1 (word instruction)
d = 1 (to reg)
v = 1 (count in CL)
x = don't care

Source: *The 8086/8088 Primer* by Stephen Morse

APPENDIX D: HEXADECIMAL AND DECIMAL CONVERSION

4		3		2		1	
HEX	= DEC	HEX	= DEC	HEX	= DEC	HEX	= DEC
0	0	0	0	0	0	0	0
1	4,069	1	256	1	16	1	1
2	8,192	2	512	2	32	2	2
3	12,288	3	768	3	48	3	3
4	16,384	4	1,024	4	64	4	4
5	20,480	5	1,280	5	80	5	5
6	24,576	6	1,536	6	96	6	6
7	28,672	7	1,792	7	112	7	7
8	32,768	8	2,048	8	128	8	8
9	36,864	9	2,304	9	144	9	9
A	40,960	A	2,560	A	160	A	10
B	45,056	B	2,816	B	176	B	11
C	49,152	C	3,072	C	192	C	12
D	53,248	D	3,328	D	208	D	13
E	57,344	E	3,584	E	224	E	14
F	61,440	F	3,840	F	240	F	15

INDEX

C

D

E

F

G

H

I

J

K

L

M

N

O

P

R

S

T

U

W

Z

ORDER FORM FOR

PROGRAM LISTINGS ON DISKETTE

This diskette contains the complete program listings for all programs and applications contained in this book. By using this diskette, you will eliminate time spent typing in pages of program code.

If you did not buy this book with diskette, use this form to order now:

Only:
$20.00

MANAGEMENT INFORMATION SOURCE, INC.
1107 N.W. 14th • Portland, Oregon 97209

NAME (Please print or type) ______________________

ADDRESS ______________________

CITY ______________ STATE ______ ZIP ______

Call free
1-800-MANUALS

☐ *Assembly Language Interfacing Diskette only $20.00*

Please add $2.00 for shipping and handling.

Please check

☐ *VISA* ☐ *MasterCharge* ☐ *American Express*

☐ *Check enclosed $*______

ACCT. ______________________

EXP. DATE ______________________

SIGNATURE ______________________

MIS: PRESS

MANAGEMENT INFORMATION SOURCE, INC.